Terry,

  Peace, Love and many
Daisies to you on your
journey of the heart,

FOLLOWING
DAISIES

A True Story About

One Woman's Adventures

Finding Happiness, Fulfilling Dreams

& Becoming Herself

HEATHER PARDON

Dedicated to
the dreamer in each of us...

"Follow your heart, wherever it takes you"
Miss Daisy

table of contents

introduction

By 2008, I'd reached the point that many of us reach in life. I had a "normal" life that included a nice house in a nice neighbourhood in a nice city, a respectable work life, numerous possessions and a busy social life. But I wasn't happy. In fact, I didn't even like my life.

I had been very busy trying to find happiness and fulfilment in an existence that truly wasn't my own design. *This isn't me,* I thought, feeling like misfit in my own life. Somewhere in the midst of that seemingly comfortable existence, I was beginning to feel extremely *un*comfortable.

"I'm reading *The Alchemist* by Paulo Coelho," said my houseguest Roberto over breakfast one morning back in August 2008. "You should read it. I think you'd really enjoy it."

Some latent instinct told me that this was no casual recommendation, but rather one of those moments in life that called for my *full* attention. Life was speaking to me and Roberto, the messenger, had just passed along the message. While I'd never heard of *The Alchemist* before I purchased the book the next day. I couldn't put the book down until I'd finished reading it—from cover to cover late that same evening. A force from within its pages had pierced my heart and found my soul, and was tantalizing me with the tales of Santiago's adventures.

The Alchemist is a fable about Santiago, a shepherd boy who leaves behind the life he knows in Spain to follow his heart and his dreams across the deserts of Egypt. I instinctively felt I'd found a soul mate in Santiago and his story. *Heather, follow your heart. Have faith and don't worry. Life always watches over us and rewards those who take risks.*

Ten months later, I would set off on an unplanned journey much like Santiago's, leaving my usual life behind to hit the road in my RV, *Miss Daisy,* heading west across Canada to see where my heart would lead me.

It seemed in the months following my meeting with Roberto that life was calling to me. *Heather, you need a change. A big change.*

What did I want? I wanted to follow my heart in every aspect of my life, just like Santiago did, and see what would happen. I'd ignored my heart many times in the past, to my own detriment, now I was ready and willing to listen to its voice and its wisdom.

In July 2009, after saying goodbye to my familiar life, I hit the road in *Miss Daisy*, on my own personal quest. *What would I find on my journey of the heart? Would I find happiness? Would I connect with my reason for being on this Earth? Would I find Me? Would I fulfil some of my dreams? Would I finally be able to create a life that I love?*

The message emblazoned on the side of *Miss Daisy* summed up my mantra for my pilgrimage: *Follow Your Heart, Wherever It Takes You.* My plan was simple. To leave town with no firm plan, no road map and no set itinerary. My only 'goal' was to keep following the wild daisies that seemed to have lined the roadside of my life the past few years, like signposts directing the way.

It is likely no small coincidence that wild daisies are my flower. They're a vibrant, happy wanderer, a flower with a simple life purpose—to thrive in the wild, to spread joy and to help nurture the growth of other wild daisies.

Reactions from my friends and family to my wandering plans were unanimous. "You're crazy," or "I would love to do that...," as their thoughts ventured off into dreams of their own. Moments later, more often than not, this was followed by the words," but I can't."

"Why not?" I would ask and a long list of reasons generally followed. We can be our own dreams worst enemies, killing them before they get to take even their first breath!

Life had beckoned me for whatever reason. While many things were uncertain, of these three things I was very sure. I needed to listen to the call of my heart. I needed to trust the wisdom of the wild daisies in my life. And I needed to share my story about what happens when you follow your heart wherever it takes you.

chapter 1

felt quite silly driving around a giant Daisymobile called 'Mr. Daisy' so this RV cultural norm worked in my favour.

I remember driving her away that day and thinking: *Wow Heather, you've really gone and done it now!* In less than two months, I'd gone from owning an ordinary stationary house with its rather stationary existence to driving a house on wheels and launching a gypsy-like lifestyle.

Excitement flooded my brain cells as I sat behind the wheel of *Miss Daisy*. I inhaled a deep breath of freedom. Parts of me that had been dormant for years popped up, peeking out of their burrows to see what was going on. I sensed that the road ahead would somehow give birth to my dreams, let fresh air blow into my life and open the doors to new possibilities.

It had been 40 years since I'd said the words, "I want to be a truck driver," yet my dream had never left my heart, nor it seems had the folks at Magical Dream Place Headquarters forgotten about it. In fact, they had magically found a way to transform my dream into something beyond my imagination. My dream rocked! I wasn't simply going to be a truck driver, I was going to be a Daisymobile driver, adventuring across Canada in my giant daisy machine.

It seemed that everything had come together beautifully. There was just one small detail to tend to.

I had yet to tell my Mom that I'd bought a 'house.'

chapter 2

The Somewhat Spontaneous House Sale

"I'm selling my house," I told my friend in the spring of 2009. Then the shocked questions began.

"What? When did you decide this? What about your bed and breakfast? What are you going to do about that? Where are you going to live? Are you going to buy another house? Why are you selling?" my panicked friend asked. I soon learned that I didn't need to worry because I would have plenty of friends and family who seemed happy to worry on my behalf.

"Well, I wasn't thinking about selling, then one thing lead to another and now there's a For Sale sign on my front yard. It probably seems a bit sudden, but it just feels right. I don't know yet what I'm going to do. I'll see how life unfolds from here," I explained, sort of.
My stunned friend looked at me as if my head had turned into a melon, struggling to comprehend why I'd leave behind my familiar life. I hadn't lost my mind, I assured her, I was simply beginning to find my heart.

~

The previous Wednesday had begun like most other Wednesdays did. I awoke early and served breakfast to the guests who were currently staying at my bed and breakfast. Wednesdays were often Waffle Day around the Wild Daisy B and B, a sweet day of carbohydrate-loaded alliteration for my guests. After breakfast, a morning workout and a few errands, it would seem that life decided that it was time to shake things up a bit.

My friend Peggy called to invite me over to see a new house that she and her husband had just put an offer on. With my answer of, "Yes, I'd love to see the house," I set off a cascading domino effect of events that quickly led to the rather unscheduled sale of my own house, rapid sell-off of most of my worldly possessions, an unplanned purchase of a 27-foot recreational vehicle and the beginning of a complete life overhaul. Saying 'yes' can have that kind of effect on one's life! It also seems to be the one word that activates the signal to the folks at Magical Dream Place Headquarters.

"Hey everyone, it's time for Heather's Dream Train to leave the station. She said yes, she's ready to go!"

~

I'd purchased my house in downtown Ottawa a few years back in 2003. It was a cute, semi-detached home on a quiet heritage street, the kind of home that many aspire to own. It was the first house that I'd ever purchased and I had fallen in love with it at first sight.

2009, I was contacted by Grace, a feng shui practitioner who was planning a visit to Ottawa. My feng shui prayer had been answered and we quickly bartered a deal. In exchange for a stay at my bed and breakfast, Grace offered me a feng shui consultation on my home.

Grace, the person, and Grace, the divine force, entered into my life with most synchronous timing. Both arrived the day that I signed the papers that secured the deal on the sale of my house. The ink had barely dried on the deal when Grace began, "So tell me about your experience in this house."

Grace lived up to her name. She had a calm, confident energy and an aura of divinity that surrounded her. There was no doubt that I'd come face to face with my feng shui master.

I shared my long list of experiences in the house, many of which seemed likely fodder for a reality television show. Besides the aforementioned relationship meltdown and ill-timed mid-July death of my refrigerator that left my house smelling like rotten salmon for weeks, there were the numerous costly home repairs and the crazy student tenants. There were also a few 'memorable' B and B guests including the obsessive-compulsive man who scrubbed and bleached the bathroom walls, resulting in the need for a revised paint job, and the fellow who completely misread my leisure interests and invited me to his friend's nudist camp. There was the guest who punched a hole in the wall. Life did not always run smoothly shall I say.

Grace listened without judgement, only nodding as I continued my story. When I finished she simply said, "I can understand why this house didn't work out for you." She pointed out areas of my home where objects were misplaced, places that needed enhancement, but most importantly, she helped me to begin to understand the importance of energy in my life. What surrounds me, whether people, places or things, not only impacts my life but also serves as a reflection of what is going on within it. I'd been surrounded by turmoil, discontent and stress for years. Clearly, it was time to have a look at what was going on inside of me.

I felt wiggly-giggly with excitement. There was no doubt that selling my house was the right thing to do. Not that I'd left myself with any other option at that point anyways!

The first thing I needed to do was to deal with my 'stuff'. We can become inexplicably attached to our 'stuff'. I would guess that most of us don't even know what 'stuff' we actually have. We are a culture that strives for it, longs for it, places inexplicable value on it, yet one that also has a lack of awareness of the impact of our 'stuff'.

I had accumulated a two-storey, three-bedroom house full of stuff in less than six years. I'll admit that I felt somewhat nervous as I glanced around the living room, trying to choose one object to part ways with. This would mark the beginning of my process of letting go and saying goodbye to the place I'd called home for the past six years. Grace guided my choice: "Choose something you haven't used in the past year. Or something you use only seasonally. Or something you don't feel particularly attached to."

A candle on the fireplace mantle caught my eye. I didn't truly like the candle; it was merely taking up some space that I once thought needed to be filled.

I didn't love it, my inside voice reminded me. I had never even used it. *Heather, fill your life with things you love.* I put it into a box, wondering why I'd kept it so long, the first item of many that I would let go of in the weeks and months to come.

There was one last piece of advice that Grace left me with. "You need to face west in order to prosper in all areas of your life." The messenger and the message had arrived. Somehow, west it would be.

~

We're taught that life is linear, A goes to B, B leads to C, and so on. Thus when I sold my house, I followed convention and began the search for another. I looked at homes for a few weeks without having any luck finding whatever it was I was searching for.

My search ended one day when my agent showed me the 'Westmount', a model home in the west side of the city. Something about that house left me feeling a sense of warmth and excitement I'd not felt in a long time. As we were about to leave, I was stopped in my tracks as I glanced into the powder room and smiled. Staring back at me were two large pictures of wild daisies, a flower that seemed to line the roadside of my life. My search for a new house stopped then and there, even though the model home was not yet on the market for sale. There was just something about the 'Westmount' that had captured my attention and left me no reason to search any further.

Meanwhile, my family and friends kept up their vigil of worry and concern.

"Are you looking for a house?" they'd ask.

"No."

"Well, where are you going to live?"

"I don't know, don't worry about it." I extend my apologies to all those, particularly my mother, for whom my replies likely caused a shortening of life span.

What I felt like doing and what made the most sense to me was simply to continue getting rid of unwanted stuff in my life. When I looked back on my life and my house, it was like looking back at a burning building. I couldn't escape fast enough.

It wasn't until five weeks away from my June 24 closing date that I decided it was time to figure out where I was going to live next.

And that's when I called my friend Tara.

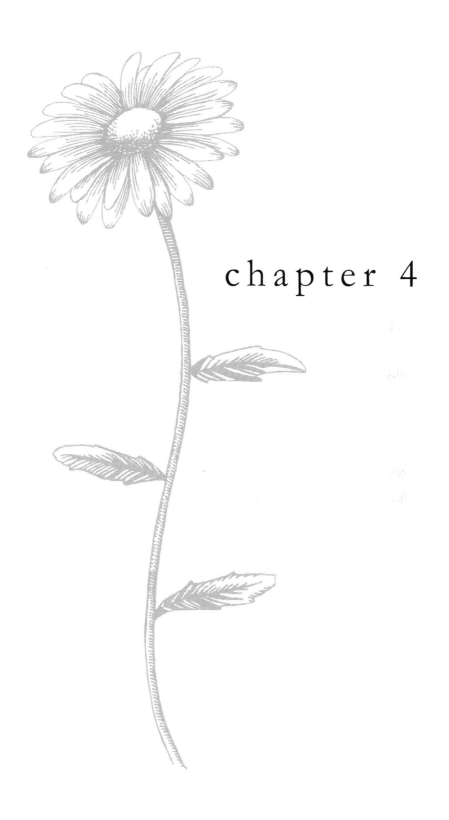

chapter 4

Intuitively Speaking

I sensed that 2008 was going to be a very different kind of year. It began innocuously enough that January, with its usual pattern of normalcy. One week I was blissfully unaware and enjoying bonbons on the couch while watching *Friends* reruns. A few weeks later, a wacky series of synchronous life events unfolded that landed me in a church basement, studying the poetry of Rumi amidst Sufi Masters and pondering large existential life questions. Something strange, powerful and very new was going on in my life and I wasn't sure exactly what it was. I needed some insight. I decided that if there was ever a year for me to see a psychic, 2008 would be the year.

Shortly after this mystical uprising in my life began, my friend Peggy offered me a tantalizing opportunity. It was only the second time we'd met when she said, "What are you doing next Friday? Would you like to go on a Caribbean Cruise? I have some free tickets to give away. "

These kinds of offers don't come along every day but even when they do, once the initial excitement passes we tend to veer quickly back to the practicalities of life.

My Brush with Grace

Feng shui. I could barely pronounce the term, but for some reason in the months prior to selling my house, I suddenly developed an interest in it.

No, it's not an oriental noodle dish. Feng shui does have its origins in the Eastern world however. Let me clearly state that I am not a feng shui expert by any means. On the other hand, I do make a very nice pad thai which would be helpful if we were discussing noodles but we're not. My understanding of feng shui is this—it's a rather mystical and complex body of knowledge that shows us how to balance the energies of any given space to help assure our health and good fortune.

How were my surroundings impacting me? I'd begun to wonder. *Could I incorporate feng shui into my own life and achieve different results?* I'd heard stories of folks who'd integrated the principles of feng shui only to see their business profits increase or to attract new love. At the very least, I figured it might help me locate a few pairs of missing socks or take my pad thai to even greater heights.

I suspect that the gang at the Magical Dream Place Headquarters had something to do with how it happened. Earlier in the spring of

chapter 3

idea. Five days later, much to everyone's surprise, including my own, there was a For Sale sign out front of my house as well as several question marks lingering on the horizon of life.

Taking leaps of faith in life was not foreign to me, but this was the biggest and perhaps craziest leap in Heather Pardon history. It had all happened so quickly. I hadn't really thought about the fact that I'd made a decision that would render me 'homeless' and out of business in one fell swoop. I barely had time to settle my own questioning before the onslaught of questions came from family, friends and neighbours. I had veered off the path of normal and it seemed that everyone was checking in to see whether I'd noticed the untravelled path beneath me.

I didn't know all the answers to the questions. As the days went on however, I began to feel at peace with my decision. I began to think about the expenses and upkeep of my house. I realized I'd always struggled financially within its walls. My relationships had never succeeded. I didn't even like the house anymore. Most importantly, *I didn't even like the life I was living.* I had merely been tolerating it. I wanted to love my life and everything in it. I was more than ready for a change.

Thankfully, change happened quickly. Three weeks later, my house sold.

that those two things cannot occur simultaneously. From the outside looking in, I had a nice life filled with all the things we somewhat naively expect will bring us happiness. Yet from the inside looking out, the picture was very different.

I'd begun to build up a mound of debt and felt financially drained. My businesses weren't thriving. I no longer felt passionate about my work. The responsibility of keeping up the house often left me feeling overwhelmed and exhausted. I was working hard and not getting any further ahead. I might have been content but I wasn't truly happy.

I just didn't know what to do about anymore. Fortunately, that's when life stepped in and helped me out with the answer once again.

~

When Peggy invited me over to see her prospective house in 2009, a voice inside of me said 'yes' without hesitation. As we toured the gorgeous new home, she turned to me and said, "Heather, the house across the street is for sale too, why don't you have a look at it?" The thought of living across the street from one of the most fun people I know seemed to be as good a reason as any to have a look at the house.

Maybe there was a secret ingredient in the waffles that morning, I don't recall. I only know that at some point between dawn and dusk that fateful Wednesday, selling my house began to seem like a great

As it often does, life kindly nudged me in the direction I needed to go next. My friend Jackie was visiting one day and suggested that I could open a bed and breakfast. The thought had never crossed my mind before, but she'd now planted the seed of an idea (bad pun in a book about daisies, I know, but hey, it works) and I seriously considered the possibility. The more that I thought about it, the more it made sense to me. I felt dissatisfied in my current job and began to realize that I needed to do work that fuelled my soul. Either that or I needed to be prepared to spent the rest of my days wondering about what might have been.

Two years later, I found the courage to leave behind my stable job and open: A Wild Daisy Bed and Breakfast in 2006. The whole daisy thing was now beginning to grow and spread even further.

~

It wasn't easy but it was a move in the right daisy direction for a while. Financially, the house continued to be a stretch for me. With my partner out of the picture, my share of the mortgage doubled and hefty maintenance and repair bills often left my bank account on the wafer-thin side. Nonetheless, I did what I could to keep going. I welcomed bed and breakfast guests, boarded short-term students in the off-season and juggled work as a personal trainer as well as a part-time job to keep my homeowner's dream afloat.

I somehow thought that living this life would bring me happiness and satisfy the expectations of those around me. I'm fairly certain now

It was on a drive up to Whistler from Vancouver that we decided to give each other nicknames and pseudo-professions. Our usual names and professions just seemed a wee bit too 'normal' for the purposes of our trip. We brainstormed with the words that appeared on roadside signs. The highway sign that pointed to Daisy Creek provided the inspiration for the nickname that I would carry from that day forward—*Daisy*. I was no longer the Heather Pardon I once knew. I welcomed my alter ego, 'Daisy, Pet Psychologist' for the week.

~

I happily returned home with my new Daisy identity, which added a much-needed element of fun to my life. A few daisies also began to pop up in my surroundings too as friends gifted me with decorative daisy items for my home. I'd closed the door on a painful phase of life only to open the next door and be greeted by this vibrant yellow and white flower. Daisies seemed to signal hope, a fresh start of some sort and perhaps a change in the course of my own destiny.

In the weeks and months that followed, I found some sort of peace and healing in transforming my surroundings. I painted the entire house, bringing new joy into the space with rich, vibrant colours on the walls. I enjoyed shopping for and refurbishing older furniture. I decorated. I built a front porch and put in a garden complete with wild daisies. I put my stamp on the house and made it mine. Life continued to be a struggle in many other ways though and to add another item onto my list of things that weren't working in my life, I'd also reached the point where I felt miserably unhappy in my job.

2003 had going for it was the occasional good hair day, stress-induced weight loss and the therapeutic healing I found at the nearest Dairy Queen.

It was in those mentally bleak days however, that life also granted me one of my greatest gifts, another 'yes' moment. I dearly needed a holiday that summer. It was at a mountain bike race one weekend where I met up with fellow members of my women's racing team, Nancy and Jenn. They were planning a trip to a race in Whistler, British Columbia the following month with another team member. "Would I like to join them?" they casually asked.

Did I dare? With finances tight, anyone with left-brained accounting skills would have told me not to go on the trip. I barely knew any of these women and would be spending a week in together close quarters. As I pondered the decision one afternoon, I glanced up at my bulletin board to see a fortune cookie quote I had pinned there: *Let Your Heart Guide You.* Generally speaking, I would not advocate making key life decisions according to what you find inside your fortune cookie, but it seemed like the wisdom that I needed at the time.

I needn't have worried about the trip. The four of us quickly and easily became good friends. Within days, we were posing in our bras atop the Whistler town welcome sign, but that's a whole other story I'll save for another time. Our many laughs and shared adventures provided the life therapy that I desperately needed.

I bought the house with my partner at the time. Love, or what I thought was love, was blind in my case and our joint purchase of the house only served to reveal more cracks in the rocky foundation of our already unhealthy relationship. The move brought with it a new form of chaos into my life, a palpably negative energy that escalated with each day. A mere three weeks after we'd moved in, our relationship ended the evening I was physically assaulted and my partner was removed from the house in handcuffs.

Even adversity has a bright side. I had been given a wakeup call and an opportunity for a fresh start. When two police cruisers arrive at your door at 3 a.m., lights flashing and sirens blaring, you have to begin to ask yourself some tough questions. *How did I get here? When did I stop listening to my inner truth? Why did I settle for less than I wanted and deserved?*

I was lost and the first step would involve unravelling everything that led me to this place where my life and my Self were not nearly what I'd imagined nor wanted them to be.

~

In the weeks that followed, I muddled through the fog that was my life at the time. I tried to enjoy being a new homeowner in those first few months despite the roof springing a leak, both the oven and refrigerator dying and the water heater flooding the basement. At the same time, I stressed over the legalities of the situation with my former partner. It seemed that the only thing that the Summer of

chapter 5

Freedom Day

In late spring 2009, I'd begun searching for a camper van of my own, the hippie within wanted a VW Westphalia. An inner voice however told me that I wouldn't find my camper until the deal on my house had closed. I don't know why, but I don't think life allows us to hang onto two things at once. You can't have the house filled with contradictory energy that caused so much turmoil and pain, and also have your new dream home. It just doesn't work that way.

The rate at which I began to empty my house had also increased significantly. I was willing, ready and able to let go of much in life. I gave away, sold or donated items, emptying my house of possessions with the same ferocity that most folks reserve for Boxing Days sales. My neighbours loved me as every day I had new offerings at the curb, ready for them to take away to their homes.

Many of us find joy, or think we do, in the accumulation of possessions and stuff. Yet, I found even greater joy in getting rid of most of mine, except for those items that I treasured deeply which were headed for my storage unit. I heeded Grace's advice on that. Many friends asked whether it was difficult to get rid of my things. It wasn't. Most of my items went to ideal owners, people who would treasure them, needed them or couldn't afford new. I found a friend who'd lost her job and was in need of a desk. Other items went to a woman who was recovering from an abusive relationship and starting over in life. A neighbour made a point to drop by and tell me how wonderfully my antique lamp fit into her surroundings. Some items went to a shelter for men rebuilding their lives in the wake of homelessness. I found people who would value my items more than I had or ever would. I was simply beginning to value different things in life.

On one hand, getting rid of my household 'stuff' was the easy part. It would be ridding myself of the large amount of unresolved emotional 'stuff' I'd gathered over the years that would be far more difficult. You can't sell that stuff at a garage sale or leave it at the curb for your neighbours.

~

"I've recently sold my house, rid myself of most of my possessions and I'm going to buy a camper van and travel out west." I said to my no-nonsense friend Pat as I had a brief meltdown on the phone. The day before I'd come home after dropping off the first load of my 'must keep' items at my storage unit. As I walked in the front door, I collapsed into tears, caught off guard by the watershed of unidentified emotions that had set themselves free.

"I'm excited about my adventure so why do I feel like an emotional train wreck?" I asked Pat.

"You need to go see Tony, he can help you," she simply advised. I wasn't even sure what I needed help with, but I always trusted Pat's advice. She just seemed to know things.

~

Tony is a feng shui practitioner, vibrational healer and tuning-fork practitioner. He greeted me with a huge smile, wearing a bright Hawaiian print shirt and infused with such positive, electric energy that I wasn't sure if his feet were actually touching the ground. Aloha! I'd met my healer.

Up until that point in my life, I'd generally considered forks to be a dining utensil. In this case, however, Tony would be using his tuning forks and intuitive powers to clear energy blockages, fix up my chakras, summon the help of my spirit guides, raise my vibration and hopefully make the crying fits go away. I like to think of it this way. Life is a bit like a dance floor and I was still being a wallflower, not quite ready to show the world my moves. Tony would help me bring my energy out onto the dance floor so that I could begin to do my own dance of life.

Our body stores the energy of our past experiences in ways and places that we aren't even aware of. And if it's not good energy, it's like having party poopers right inside of you! Over the next few sessions together Tony would sound his tuning forks, holding them over different parts of my body as he let the vibration from the fork work on my energy and release some unwanted guests from my life party.

There were many to be banished. Some had overstayed their welcome. Some had snuck in the back door. Some were talking behind my back. Some I didn't even know. Most I tried to ignore politely, hoping they'd quietly leave from a side door. They'd put a damper on my party for far too long, these unresolved emotions, false expectations, limiting beliefs, unjustified fears, feelings of unforgiveness and more. All of their friends and relatives seemed to have crashed my party too. One by one, Tony helped summon a few bouncers who escorted them out of my life.

~

The Day from Hell. Those were the words I'd used to remember June 24 for the past six years. It was, after all, the anniversary of my former partner's arrest. It was a day I'd recalled as one of my darkest. I loathed its return each year, a reminder of a period in my life and an experience that I didn't care to remember.

I awoke on June 24, 2009, and glanced around an empty house. I was leaving the home I once thought I'd never leave. I was letting go of the house I'd fought so hard for. I was abandoning all the sweat equity I'd put into it. It seemed surreal to leave, but I was not sad to go. After touring the house one last time, gathering the last of my belongings and bidding farewell, I was happy to close the door on that house and that chapter of my life.

I then headed over to my appointment with Tony.

~

"It's no coincidence that the stars aligned to close the deal on your house on this day. Life is giving you a chance to see June 24 in a new light," Tony began.

I had just closed one door and I could already feel the next one slowly begin to open.

"We're going to work on your solar plexus, that's the centre of control," he said. I found that rather coincidental on a day that I'd long associated with a complete lack of control. The spirits were telling me something. *Make June 24 **your** day, Heather.*

I needed to let go, Tony told me. The weight of negative emotions from that relationship and the events of June 24 had burdened me all those years. I couldn't move forward and continue to carry that load with me.

Tony worked patiently with me that day, slowly removing the piles of damaging emotional debris that had accumulated. As the tuning fork sent healing vibrations through my body, the spirits surrounding us offered messages. For two and a half hours, Tony gently coached me forward and yet I continued to feel stuck somewhere.

Help.

"What do you need to do?" he softly asked. A wee light glimmered beyond my slightly ajar door.

I need to forgive.

I hadn't forgiven my former partner. I had never felt the need to forgive. And perhaps I'd never wanted to forgive. More importantly, I hadn't forgiven myself for playing a role in such a dysfunctional relationship. I hadn't known or understood that it would be through forgiveness that I would eventually find my freedom. It was so clear to me in that moment, but why hadn't it come to me before?

It can be comfortable to hang onto things, even if they are no longer serving us. The alternative can feel daunting. It was time for me to release the burden of the anger, negativity and guilt I'd carried with me for far too long. I visualized myself in a tug of war with this trio and at one point, I simply let go of the rope, releasing myself from my emotional captors. *What a huge relief.* I felt a huge internal void, one that I could now fill with great things, positive things.

A new day with a new meaning had dawned. I'd closed the door on a chapter of my life. I finally bid farewell to the June 24 I once knew and welcomed a powerful new June 24 into my life, 'Freedom Day'.

And the very next day, I found my camper.

chapter 6

On Finding *Miss Daisy*

When you're about to embark on the adventure of a lifetime, then a traditional motor home will simply not do. Thus, I'd begun my search for a camper by looking for a Volkswagen Westphalia, the much-revered hippie camper of the '60s and '70s.

The Westphalia subculture is unique and even as a Birkenstock-wearing, environmentally conscious, peace-minded daisy lover, I quickly learned that I would not be granted immediate access.

"What would you be doing with the camper?" asked one owner, as I examined his used Westphalia. I suspected that he did not want to hear that I'd be heading to the nearest provincial park every weekend to bask in a comfortable camping experience.

"I've recently sold my house and got rid of my worldly possessions as I no longer wish to feed the capitalist machine. I intend to spend the rest of my days countering traditional cultural norms, fighting the establishment and eating a completely organic, granola-based diet. There is also a good chance I'll be putting some daisy decals on the camper."

He smiled, apparently pleased with my answer.

After a few weeks of searching, I never had any luck finding a Westphalia, however. It seems that life decided that it just wasn't enough "truck" for me and my lifelong truck-driving dream.

 The day was June 25. Only a few nights earlier I'd been enjoying dinner with my friend Reta when I mentioned I'd be leaving on my trip mid-July, even though I'd not yet procured a suitable RV. I had somehow figured that life would handle that small detail for me. Call it synchronicity or call it the side effects of a delicious pasta primavera and a few glasses of wine, but Reta suddenly recalled that she knew of a friend who was selling her RV. Four days later I found myself standing in front of the future *Miss Daisy*.

She wasn't glamorous at first sight yet she had an allure about her that intrigued me. Perhaps it was our commonalities that appealed to me. She was an "older model" and had clearly been around the block a few times. Like myself, she came with a few wrinkles and scratches, signs of a life well lived, yet she seemed comfortable in her own skin. From her parking spot in the driveway she seemed as discontent with her stationary existence as I had been with mine. "I'm ready for an adventure, I'm ready to hit the open highway," she seemed to be saying. I had found a kindred RV spirit.

Her inner beauty revealed even more of her character. From the off-pink decor to the 1980s velour sofa, she'd kept her original parts, never having changed a thing about herself. Here was a woman who knew who she was and was confident sharing her true self with the world. She had much to offer—a vast living space, kitchen, stove, refrigerator, bathroom, shower and a double bed—all the comforts of home. In my eyes, she was as complete as an RV could be, the perfect role model and ally for my trip.

Next came time to sit in the cockpit of her mightiness and admire the view. It was like sitting in a comfortable living room recliner on the top of the world. I felt as commanding as Captain Kirk at the helm of the Star ship *Enterprise*. I felt exhilarated, in control of my galaxy and completely empowered as I took her for a drive. Be damned any Klingon or pesky mosquito who would dare try to overthrow my vessel!

I was in love. She was 'The One' and I agreed to return a few days later to pay for the RV and whisk her away to a new life.

There was only one small glitch. I still needed the money to pay for her.

~

By this point, I'd begun to take note of a recurring pattern in my life, which I called, 'The 11th Hour Bailout'. The 11th Hour Bailout occurred on a fairly frequent basis, generally as I stepped out onto new limbs in life. There'd I'd be, inching further and further along the limb, feeling some trepidation and uncertainty as to how the story may end, when life would suddenly swoop in like a Superhero and provide The 11th Hour Bailout, that safety net that would allow me to continue to move outward along the limb.

The purchase of my RV would be another one of those Bailout situations. I did not have a large, well-padded, offshore bank account to finance my trip. The proceeds from the sale of my house would be my *modus financus operandi* to pay for my new rig, settle some debts and take care of the rest of my adventure. You may then wonder why I'd agreed to purchase an RV before I actually had the cheque from my lawyer. Things out on this new limb just seemed to be working so I had to trust that this piece of the puzzle would drop into place somehow as well.

At noon on the agreed-upon pickup date, I headed to my lawyer's office to enquire about my funds.

"Funny to see you here," she greeted me, "I was just about to give you a call. Your cheque is ready." I simply smiled at the 11th hour manner in which my life Superheroes had brought this all together. *Whew.* I'd even been left enough time to get a bank draft and arrive on schedule at 2 p.m. to pick up my rig. *Thanks guys. Perhaps with a few more lessons in faith I could graduate to the 10th Hour Bailout Program someday?*

~

As we enjoyed a cold beer together, Sue, the former RV owner, gave me a quick overview as to the inner and outer workings of my new rig. I nodded, pretending to understand, as she spoke about generators, various batteries and charging systems, holding tanks, propane things, and waste and water management. *Did Captain Kirk have to concern himself with these kinds of details?*

I was far too excited to worry about learning about the mechanical intricacies of my rig. There would be plenty of time for that later. All I could think about was the sense of freedom that I enjoyed as I gazed at the road ahead of me and dreamed of the many adventures that awaited.

As Sue handed me the keys and I prepared to drive away in my new dream home, I glanced to the side of the driveway where I noticed a lovely patch of wild daisies growing next to my rig. I smiled at the auspicious send off to my journey and the message they seemed to say. *Go Heather. Be free. Be a wild daisy. Enjoy. And don't worry, this isn't the last you'll see of us. We'll be with you all the way.*

chapter 7

Look Mom, I Bought an RV!

She was sitting in the living room knitting when I walked in the front door that day. I'd just made the four-hour journey to my Mom's house to show her my new rig. *Miss Daisy* was parked just out of sight of the front window for full surprise effect.

This wouldn't be the first time that I'd surprised my Mom with a significant shift in my life. There was the time that I dyed my hair bleach blonde days before my cousin's wedding, or the time I quit my job unexpectedly, or the day I surprised her with the purchase of my new SUV or the time I suddenly informed her, "Hey, I'm moving to Ottawa." As the person who birthed me into the world, I reasoned that it simply came with the territory for her to be able to flow with my moments of randomness.

"Hi Mom, I just bought a new house!"

Her face lit up with pride and excitement as she asked, "where?"

"It's parked outside," I replied. Her knitting came to a complete halt, which I knew was a bad sign. Mom would continue to knit while a tornado passed through town if it meant she'd get to finish another pair of mittens.

In recent weeks, conversations with my Mom often went like this:

Mom: "So where are you looking for a new house?"

Me: "I'm not looking."

Mom: "So where are you going to live?"

Me: "Don't worry Mom, I'll be just fine."

Mom: "Gosh, you need a house!"

Me: "Did I mention that I'd be just fine?"

I could sense that Mom didn't really like my answers. And although she never specified so, I think she meant that she wanted me to have a 'traditional' house, as in one that wasn't on wheels.

~

I took her outside and introduced her to *Miss Daisy*. There were long pauses of silence in those first few minutes as she pondered the thought of her youngest daughter driving across Canada in an RV. For a few minutes I wondered whether she was going to try to ground me at the age of 46. No doubt she likely spent those minutes also wondering where the daisy she'd gone wrong that I ended up without the familial lawyer or accountant gene.

As she looked over *Miss Daisy*, thoughts of her wandering gypsy daughter's lifestyle dancing through her head, she uttered her first words, "But you're going to buy a house at some point, aren't you?"

"Yes Mom, I'll buy a house … someday."

And with those words, I knew that I wouldn't be grounded.

~

"Mom, put down your knitting. We're going for a ride in *Miss Daisy*," I said to her the next morning. At 79, Mom had never been in an RV before. It's nice to know that even as we grow older we can still have some 'firsts' to look forward to.

Mom rode shotgun in the passenger seat and as we toured the neighbourhood, she proclaimed the ride to be very comfortable. From my vantage point on the driver's side, she seemed to enjoy riding up so high, enjoying the open view and feeling the power of being in such a big rig.

While my Mom didn't say much I saw a smile flash across her lips as she disembarked from *Miss Daisy*. It was the first smile I'd seen on her face since she'd met *Miss Daisy*. I think it was the smile of someone who'd just tasted adventure.

Maybe we weren't that different after all. Perhaps beneath all that knitting was a woman who understood my yearning and my need to wander. Maybe there was even a part of her that enjoyed adventure too. And who knows, maybe there'd be a part of me that would want a traditional house again someday. Just not yet.

chapter 8

Saying My Goodbyes

I had never imagined leaving behind a comfortable life, friends and family to wander off into the sunset in a giant Daisymobile.

The funny thing about embracing our dreams is that we never know how they're going to unfold. I had no idea that my childhood truck-driving dream would later morph into a cross-Canada, soul-searching journey. I also didn't know that it would involve letting go of so much of my past and saying some difficult goodbyes.

At times it felt as if I was falling into a void. I was letting go of things even though nothing new had yet entered my life to take its place. It was often similar to that frightening falling sensation you experience at the top of the roller coaster, just as you are about to take a big plunge. You hover and then freefall for a few seconds in that in-between space before you come up the other side, thankfully arriving safely and exhilerated. I yearned for that kind of adventure yet still, it was a big change for me and one that wasn't always easy. As my departure date approached, the time also came to say goodbye to friends I wouldn't be seeing for several months. I am a fairly social person so it was somewhat difficult to look ahead at the unknown solo adventure that lay before me. As much as I was excited about the journey, there is comfort in being surrounded by those you know and love.

But I'd realized that I'd reached a time in my life when I needed to walk by myself and just see what would happen. I'd spent so much of my life walking with or for others. Learning to walk comfortably in my own shoes was long overdue.

With each step out of my comfort zone, a few small twinges of fear still crept into my brain.

Will I get lonely? Will I miss home? What will I do if I get a flat tire or if my RV breaks down? Will I begin to talk to myself? What if I don't like RVing? I knew with certainty that I needn't worry about locating the nearest Tim Horton's coffee outlet as they seem to be spaced at 2.3 km intervals along every major route in the country.

My biggest underlying fear was that I'd be getting to know myself in an intimate one-on-one manner that I'd never experienced before. I was shifting from a busy, action-packed, city lifestyle to a much slower pace of spending day after day on my own. It is easy not to examine yourself too deeply when other things in life can easily distract your attention.

What will I discover? What if I find out that I don't even like myself? What will I look like yanked from the usual confines of life? What will I create? These are frightening questions to consider when you've just pulled your entire life up by its roots.

I also had to begin to say goodbye to these fears however. I used think of my fears as cautionary allies, but I began to recognize instead that they'd been holding me back for so many years. Instead, I was looking forward to getting to know some new friends along the way, like faith, trust and hope.

For every action there is an equal and opposite reaction. Such is the yin and yang of life, the forces that align to balance things. With every goodbye I said, somewhere down the road I knew there'd be a hello waiting to take its place.

chapter 9

Miss Daisy Gets
Some Feng Shui

If I wanted a different experience in life, I had to start doing things differently. Simple concept, I know, but how often do we overlook it? If I wished to fill my space with wonderful positive and adventurous energy, *Miss Daisy* would require a slight makeover. She was going to get some feng shui.

With my very limited knowledge of feng shui fundamentals, I sought the help of my friend Tony who coached me on the process and assured me that I could indeed teach an old RV some new feng shui tricks. Segmenting *Miss Daisy* into the nine areas of life, or modern bagua as it's referred to in feng shui terms, was my starting point. While I wasn't able to tell my anyone what all the batteries under the hood were for, I could certainly tell folks where my wealth and prosperity corner was!

Many people would have started off by learning the workings of *Miss Daisy* first and then focusing on the 'fluffy' stuff. I'd tried living life like that before. Being practical and living life from the outside in hadn't worked, so now I had a chance to do it differently. It was time to try living from the inside out, creating the life that I truly wanted and living authentically. I started with what matters most to me, which is living from the heart and paying attention to the energy that surrounds me. *Heather, fill your life with things you Love.* Grace's words echoed once again. There would be plenty of time to learn the mechanics of *Miss Daisy* later.

In the meantime, I filled *Miss Daisy* with things that left me feeling good, items that had meaning and purpose—photos and cards from friends, a wall hanging with a quote from the Dalai Lama about happiness and life purpose, some Winnie the Pooh trinkets, positive affirmations, and a 'radar-jamming' guardian angel who would not only ward off speeding tickets but also protect the inside of *Miss Daisy* from unwelcome odours. My baguas were looking good.

There was one small thing missing however. *Miss Daisy* was still missing some daisies.

~

The thought of leaving town without some daisies adorning the side of my rig just didn't feel right. It would have been awkward, like walking around wearing an ill-fitting pair of underpants.

With only a few days left to go to my planned departure date, I was nearly ready to give up on the idea. I hadn't found anyone who could decal my rig to suit my timeline or budget. Somewhat miraculously, a timely and synchronous conversation with my friend Pat once again pointed me in the right direction. She introduced me to a business colleague of hers who was able to complete the makeover in less than four days.

Miss Daisy became a completely transformed RV. Any woman who's had her hair or makeup done, bought a wonderful new outfit or spent a day at the spa can understand the feeling that takes place when you are transformed. Adorned in her wild daisy attire, *Miss Daisy* was beaming with newfound energy, from her roof to her tires, from her front end to her rear. I was beaming too. She was gorgeous and everything an adventurous gal could want in her RV.

We were ready to go. And just in case I would ever lose my way on our travels, the mantra on the side of *Miss Daisy* would be my constant guide: "Follow your heart, wherever it takes you."

~

With my feng shui in place, I was finally ready to tackle getting to know the operations side of *Miss Daisy*. The multitasker in me also wanted to know whether I'd be able to bake a batch of muffins and drive at the same time. I had heard of some folks who'd put their RV on cruise control while they headed to the fridge for a cold drink. I think this led to them spilling their drink. And their RV. Down an embankment. At least I knew better than that. I'd be sure to pull off to the side of the road to take my freshly baked goodies out of the oven.

When my RV-savvy friends John and Joanne offered me a private tutoring session, I gladly accepted their generous invitation to spend a Saturday afternoon reviewing RV Boot Camp 101. We powered up the generator, we looked under the hood, we turned on the oven, we opened the awning, we went through all the systems on board *Miss Daisy*.

I didn't remember much of the technical jargon for it was our conversation about poop that grabbed my attention. Proper poop management is essential to a good quality of life within your RV living quarters. You're generally travelling in the hotter summer months, you're not connected to a city sewer system, you have a holding tank to deal with ... I'm sure you're catching a whiff of what I'm talking about. At some point, you need to head to what is tastefully termed a 'dumping station' to empty your precious cargo. This is not the sexy side of RVing and there are no assistants at the dumping station to take care of matters for you. This adventure was going to force me to finally deal with my own poop in life, literally and figuratively.

"Be sure to hold the hose down firmly when you're emptying your tank otherwise the pressure can send it moving around like a snake...." As John spoke, I imagined the possible ramifications of such a mistake. It would be like the poop hitting the proverbial fan.

"This is good information," I said as I thanked John. That tip alone was worth the three- hour drive. Feeling as if I was beginning to get my RV poop together, I bid my friends goodbye. It was now time for my inaugural RV campsite experience.

~

I thought I'd reached the pinnacle of excitement when I'd pulled into the truck stop off the highway that day. *I'm in the big leagues now.* I parked my rig next to the tractor-trailers, feeling an immediate kinship. *I'd arrived.* I was finally living my truck-driving dream.
It only got more exciting the moment I pulled into my first RV campsite. I even backed *Miss Daisy* into the camping spot that day, which was no small feat. Hey, try backing up your entire house and you'll understand why I'd procrastinated on any attempts at reverse engineering.

A few minutes of fidgeting and I was hooked up to water and electricity. I then headed inside to test out a few more of the systems. Even the most mundane of tasks becomes thrilling in an RV so the excitement of vacuuming *Miss Daisy* held my attention for the next few minutes. This was later followed by the successful acquisition of hot running water and a delicious dinner prepared on the gas stove. Nothing burned. Nothing exploded. And no poop had been sprayed anywhere. So far, so good in my RV world.

~

When it came time to leave the next day, I approached the sewage hose with caution, remembering John's advice. It was Sunday morning and before breaking camp, I needed to shower and empty my tanks.

They are two tanks and two drain lines in an RV. The 'grey' tank holds water drained from the kitchen and shower. The 'black' tank holds your other worldly disposables. These need to be drained regularly and with caution as you don't want to experience the nasty, aforementioned spills in the process.

I successfully hooked up the drainage hose and emptied the black and grey water tanks without a hitch. *Whew.*

It was the water *hook-up* and hose that created havoc for me that day. As I inserted the water hose onto the attachment to fill my reserve water tank, the hose kicked back once the tank was full, spraying water everywhere and thoroughly dousing me. Wet but undaunted, I proceeded to rinse out the sewage drainage hose with the water hose. I turned the water on at the tap, completely forgetting John's advice and committing one of the classic newbie RVer mistakes. The hose moved like a snake under the pressure, dousing me with effluent once again. I would discover in the weeks and months to follow that this would not be the last time that I'd provide some amusement for the people around me.

Fortunately, I had remembered John's advice to double-check that I'd disconnected all my *hook-ups* before departing my campsite. I didn't want to be one of those people who forgot that detail and drove off site, trailing the electrical box behind.

As I performed one last check on my rig, my trailer neighbour greeted me.

"Do you drive that big thing all by yourself?" she asked. The silent voice in my head thought, *Yes, I do. Why? Are they supposed to come with a chauffeur?*

I shared with my neighbour that I would be driving *Miss Daisy* by myself, heading out west for the summer.

"Well, you're a brave woman … to do that all by yourself," she said with a tone that suggested she thought it was completely crazy of me to do so.

I didn't think of myself as brave. I was only doing what I felt was essential for me and my life. Her comments seemed to indicate however, that as a single woman driving a giant Daisymobile, I would be a bit of an oddity wherever I went.

Gone were my days of being a passenger in my own life. Gone were my days of needing to live by the rules of others. I was finally happy to be in the driver's seat. And with *Miss Daisy* as my steed, this was going to be my own journey.

chapter 10

On the Brink

It may seem strange then that I opted to kick off the start of my soul-searching adventure in Niagara Falls, arguably one of the busiest and most commercialized tourist meccas in Canada. In a town known for quick marriages, wax museums, Guinness World Record stunts and freak shows, *Miss Daisy* and I seemed incredibly conservative by comparison.

The previous summer I'd met Rob and Sherene while sharing a train ride from Toronto to Ottawa. Ebullient spirits, both of them, we connected instantly, laughing and musing about the peculiarities of life. Both Rob and Sherene had spent a number of years working in the local casino in Niagara and enthralled me with some hair-raising stories about life in the gambling world. Let me simply say that I am quite happy that my childhood days spent playing bingo in the local church basement is as far as my gambling life ever went.

Rob, who was in his early 40s, was also in the midst of a major life shift, getting ready to leave his job and head back to university. I admired and also understood his gumption. Life has a curious way of bringing people together who share similar paths. We need that. As we stand at the end of our own limb, there is comfort in looking at those around us who are also standing at the end of theirs. "'Keep going" we cheer to each other, encouragingly.

By the end of the train ride, we'd become fast friends and I invited them to cancel their hotel plans and stay at my house while in Ottawa. A few months later they returned the hospitality and I found myself parked in their driveway in Niagara Falls with *Miss Daisy*.

I had to ask myself why the universe would nudge me to head to Niagara Falls to begin my adventure. While I'd enjoyed my visits there as a young child, if not for my friendship with Rob and Sherene, a return visit as an adult would be nearly as appealing as having a root canal done.

We took the requisite ride on the *Maid of the Mist*, a small boat that takes tourists to the bottom of the Canadian falls. A trip on the *Maid* is a wonderful way to marvel at the falls' grandeur and to simulate the feeling of having a giant water balloon land on your head. I got drenched. Next on the agenda was a trip to the American falls, where we walked up and down a stairway that runs adjacent to the cascading waters. This simulated the feeling of having someone pummel us with spray from a giant water gun. I got drenched again. Soak your guests to their underwear, always a hospitable way to kick off a visit, I say.

We then headed to 'the brink' on the top end of the falls where it appeared that unless water fell from the heavens above, I'd be able to stay dry on this part of the tour. The brink is, as its name suggests, the point where the water drops over the falls.

I stood at the brink and watched the water approach, then rapidly disappear over the edge. I've never even mastered launching a cannonball off the side of the pool, I marvel at the daredevils with enough gumption (or foolishness) to plunge down the falls in a barrel. I eyed the water as it approached the brink, merrily meandering its way. As it reached the edge, it had no choice, the force of life and gravity sent it rushing headlong over the edge into the swirling waters below. There was some chaos, uncertainty and adventure as the water hurled over the edge, but eventually calm returned as it joined the river below. Its journey continued and there was a palpable peacefulness on the water as it moved on. I understood the journey of this water because it felt like my journey too.

Many days I'd spent meandering through life like water in a river. Sometimes life went smoothly, sometimes I hit rocks, sometimes I was able to avoid them and sometimes I got caught up in the current. More often than not, I felt that things weren't flowing freely or easily for me.

I eventually reached my own proverbial brink. Just as the waters of Niagara Falls couldn't fight the momentum that took them over the edge, I couldn't resist the innate forces of life that pushed me over either. The strong yearning that called me to sell my house, simplify my life and open myself to living differently had brought me to my own brink.

As I looked at the mighty Niagara and watched the waters meander downstream, with peaceful calm, I recognized why life had brought me there. *I wish to live in that flow. I wish to live in that calm.* First, I needed to understand that I had to launch myself off the brink to get myself there. And then I needed to be reassured that my jump off the brink would work out just fine too.

I'm still not sure why I needed to get drenched though.

chapter 11

If You're Roasting a Pig,
You May as Well Get Married Too

You can't be a wallflower when you're the driver of a giant
Daisymobile, I learned early on in my travels. Driving *Miss Daisy*
quickly proved to be a fun way to meet people and attract attention,
whether I wanted to or not.

I had barely arrived at my next campsite outside of Barrie, Ontario
and settled in when one of my neighbours, Nadine, stopped by and
introduced herself. Noticing that I was a lone daisy, she invited me
join her, her boyfriend, Bob and her father, Doug at their campsite
for a drink.

Not wanting to be a lone daisy for too long, I happily headed over
to their campsite. There are no boundaries or separation in camping.
Most people are just generally friendly and these folks certainly were.
I wish life was like that more often.

It turned out that they were also curious about me and *Miss Daisy*.
They'd all watched me drive in that afternoon, flaunting my daisies
and wondered if I was a cult leader, palm reader or a born-again
hippie.

"I'm forgoing the mid-life crisis thing and having a mid-life adventure instead," I replied.

Comfortably reassured that I wasn't a full-blown whacko from another daisy dimension, the beer began to flow as did the conversation.

Nadine was a single mom, with two young boys she obviously adored. She was divorced from her former husband with whom she had once shared an 8,000 sq. ft. home and a luxurious lifestyle.

"Crap doesn't bring you happiness," she offered philosophically, between puffs on her cigarette.

This piece of blunt wisdom was good to know. I was on the right track with my simpler lifestyle.

Bob worked in construction, driving heavy equipment, although he shared the fact that he'd always wanted to be a priest. He trailed off as he spoke, as if he knew he was betraying his heart in speaking those words. There was a depth and conviction to his character that suggested he'd have made a fine priest. A calm, powerful energy and an aura of helpfulness were part of his nature. Bob would be the one serving meals to the homeless or the one to rescue your cat from a burning building. I secretly wondered when he'd stopped following his dream. And, as I listened to the sadness in his voice as he spoke, I hoped he might find his way back to it again.

Doug was a cross between Santa Claus and the father from the Walton family. A friendly, burly fellow, with a soft beard and a big heart, he also had a confident calm to him. He seemed to have found some of the answers to life and shared with us some simple life truths.

He had been married twice. As we all sat and pondered our collective history of failed relationships, Doug summed up the essence of a happy relationship with some very simple wisdom.

"You should be really excited when you're on your way home to see your wife (or husband or partner)."

There was surely one of the missing ingredients in my past relationships. As simple as that.

I appreciated Doug's down-to-earth and non-conventional approach to life. All too often we inflate things to a level of false grandeur. When Doug's future second wife asked him whether he was interested in getting married, he said yes. He then informed her that he was roasting a pig the following weekend and that they could get married that day. In Doug's no-nonsense world, a pig roast provided the perfect occasion for sharing nuptials.

We were an eclectic cast of characters around the campfire that night, a soul-searching Daisymobile driver, a chain-smoking divorcee finding her way back to happiness, a wannabe priest and the sage old guy of the bunch, Santa Claus Walton. As diverse as we were, our common destiny had led our paths to serendipitously cross that day, to weave together a few more threads in the fabric of each of our lives. And perhaps to remind us all that life is really about the simple things. Like friends around a campfire, not owning too much crap, being true to ourselves or celebrating love with a pig roast. And daisies, of course. I wouldn't know any of this if it weren't for the power of daisies.

chapter 12

Life is Good

It was hard to gauge at times which part of my lifestyle some folks found crazier, my decision to venture off in an RV or my decision to live without television or newspapers.

I'd initiated the latter part in my life long before I'd met *Miss Daisy*, but maintained this hermit-like existence while we were together. I found that television and newspapers drained my energy or painted a skewed picture of the world we live in. Real life had become far more interesting, exciting and captivating for me.

This sometimes leaves me a bit behind the times on the news however. Recently, I popped a birthday card and present into the mail to my Mom and called her to see whether it had arrived yet.

"The post office went on strike two weeks ago," she informed me.

Okay, so a few things fall through the cracks from time to time, but generally it's a system that works for me.

It's not like you can't get caught up on the news (and local gossip) while waiting in line at the grocery store, chatting with your hairdresser or eavesdropping in on conversations at the local coffee shop. Many folks are happy to share news of the latest stabbings, various accidents, murders and assaults, job losses, global disasters and so on. And aren't they fun people to hang out with? Pay attention to too much of this stuff and real life may indeed start to resemble a Stephen King novel. Oftentimes these conversations are followed by comments such as "some people…….." or "I can't believe it" or "this is terrible" or "who would do such a thing?" It's a curious point of human nature that it's generally these types of things that we choose to focus on. It would be a rare occasion that you might hear some positive news. "Hey, did you hear that Betty Crocker is introducing a new cake mix?" or "Have you seen Kathy's new puppy?"

How can we feel good about ourselves or life in general if we spend so much time and energy thinking about these types of events, which, in reality, comprise a fraction of space in the whole of our world? How can we create an awesome life when we spend so much time focused on the negative? Hence, I had put myself on a media-free diet and had never felt better.

Change the way you look at things in life and the things you look at will change. I had made a conscious decision prior to my departure to embrace the belief that people come from a place of good, are willing to help and share a common destiny. I deliberately chose to believe that at the essence of human nature, we all have good and loving intentions.

Many folks asked whether I felt afraid, particularly as a woman, of travelling on my own.

"There are a lot of crazy people out there!" they'd tell me. I had to bite my tongue to stop from asking whether they were related to any of them. While I recognized that elements of danger and risk do exist in the world, I opted to focus on the positive instead. I fully expected this would also attract more positive elements and people into my life and make the days far more fun.

Life is good. People are good. Focus on the good stuff. And Life will be good.

I know that my friends and family had well-meaning intentions when they offered their cautionary warnings and thoughts. I simply chose to see the bright side and early on in my trip, when I looked around I found plenty of proof that indeed life is good.

~

Thank you God! After having spent two frustrated hours on my own trying to set up and activate my new Blackberry, on the other end of the phone line, I was greeted by the most exuberantly helpful customer service associate on the face of the earth. She may have been highly-caffeinated but whatever the reason Rebecca was in far too good of a mood to allow me to be frustrated by my Blackberry ineptitude. We enjoyed a wonderful chat, Rebecca and I, veering off topic as women are often prone to do. She was excited to tell me about her pending move out of her parents' house and I was happy to tell her a bit about my travels. Rebecca quickly became my new BBFF (Best Blackberry Friend Forever) as she was not only a great gal pal but she solved my setup issues too.

Our mutual love-in didn't end there however. With great enthusiasm, she exclaimed, "I'm going to waive the usual $35 activation fee, just because I can!" *Rebecca, could I love you any more than I already do?* It turned out that indeed I could. Only a few Blackberry newbie seconds later, I somehow mistakenly set the user language on my phone to Spanish. My knowledge of Spanish is limited to "Pass me the paella, please" so I was most grateful when Rebecca kindly helped me get de-Spanished and on my way in English again.

Rebecca went over and above 'good'. When she pushed the button on the elevator of life, it went all the way to the top floor.

~

Many well-meaning folks had also cautioned me against trusting 'strangers'. But sometimes a stranger can become a new friend. Doug, whom I'd just met at the campsite the previous night, kindly offered me a lovely parking spot at his home while I needed to stay in town to await my new awning.

"You don't need to waste money on a campsite if you don't have to," he said with his characteristic meat and potatoes take on life.

I accepted his generous offer, thanking him by cooking dinner each night. His second wife had died a few years ago and I think he simply enjoyed company. In his midst, I enjoyed a couple of nights parked under a beautiful willow tree and the opportunity to get to know him a bit better. While I learned that his tolerance for beer far surpassed mine, I also learned that he was a kind and genuine soul and not a crazy axe murderer. He was simply a 'good' man.

I imagine that either of these scenarios could have turned out differently if I'd focused my attention differently. Coincidentally enough, it seemed to be that by focusing on the positive that positive people and positive things kept coming into my life. Groovy how that works isn't it?

Life is good. At least it is when we choose to see it that way.

chapter 13

I Found a Sausage, an Apple Fritter and a Side of Faith in St. Jacobs

I raced to the door with visions of a delicious sausage on a bun dancing through my head after opportunity knocked that day. It had been years since I'd made my habitual bi-weekly trip to the St. Jacob's farmer's market in the heart of Mennonite Country. My salivary glands began drooling with anticipation the moment my friends invited me along on their road trip to the Saturday market.

Here are my words of wisdom should you ever take your own trip to St. Jacobs:

> Do not, I repeat, do not have a big breakfast before you leave home. This is not the time to start your day with oatmeal. Save your appetite for the abundance of indulgences that await you at the market.

> Leave your health conscience at home too. You won't want that nagging at you all day. Throw dietary caution to the wind as the market is an irresistible sensory fiesta. Fresh baked goods tease your nose at very turn. Rainbow displays of fresh vegetables remind you to balance your cinnamon bun intake with a green, yellow or purple veggie if you must. Beautifully made by hand

crafts are available for purchase too, once your appetite has been satisfied.

My appetite had not yet been taken care of so as soon as I arrived, I made a beeline for the line up at the legendary sausage-on-a-bun cart, home of the best sausages on the planet. They are the quinessential Cloud Nine experience complete with the sound of a choir of angels singing in your ear with every bite. Next up were the deep-fried apple fritters. Slices of fresh apple dipped in batter and gently fried in a river of slow-moving fat, then tossed in cinnamon and sugar, prepared right before your eyes. *Fry, fry, fry your apples, gently in the fat, merrily, merrily, merrily, merrily, it doesn't get better than that.* And truly, it doesn't. When I die, please, just bury me in apple fritters.

Once gastronomically and soulfully satiated, I was able to move on to other things, like hitting Main Street for some gift shopping.

As I was still seeking a few items to complete the feng shui outfitting of *Miss Daisy*, I wandered through the cornucopia of crafts. *Miss Daisy* wasn't a quiet gal shall I say; between the gentle roar of the 454 Chevy motor beneath my driver's perch and the rattling of everything in the cupboards behind, I sometimes yearned for more peace within her confines. A beautiful set of wind chimes caught my eye. Aha! They could help drown out the excess cabin noise and fill the void left by the distinct lack of radio stations along my route. At the very worst, *Miss Daisy* would sound like a giant ice cream truck and we'd receive a friendly greeting wherever we went (provided that we actually had ice cream on board, of course). I bought the chimes but decided to wait to see how things went before deciding whether to invest in an ice cream freezer too.

~

I also picked up another item that seemed essential to have on board, a reminder to help me keep the faith. After only a few days of driving around in *Miss Daisy*, I'd started to receive emails from folks who'd encountered the Daisymobile. The quote on the side of *Miss Daisy* seemed to resonate with them and I realized that I wasn't alone in my quest to find a way to live life from the heart.

Why is it so difficult to follow our heart? The main reason is due to our fears.

We fear that we might be wrong. *How do we really know what's right when it comes to something as intuitive as following our heart?*

We fear that we might fail. *What if I follow my heart and it doesn't go as I expect?*

We fear the unknown. *I don't know where my heart is going to take me! I don't know what's going to happen!*

We fear change. *I'm comfortable where I am, it's familiar to me.*

We fear that it might be difficult. *I don't want to struggle.*

We fear that we won't be able to find a good hairdresser on our travels. *Or perhaps that is just me? Now that's a story I'll save for later.*

We have all kinds of fears and can find many reasons why it's not a good idea to follow our heart. Our minds and our egos are very good at that sort of thing.

I could have come up with several of my own. *I shouldn't take the summer off to travel because we're in a recession. It's not safe for a woman to travel by herself. What if the RV breaks down? How can I afford this trip? What will I do when I get back? Where will I live?*

In moments of stillness however, we can tune into our inner voice as it speaks of desire and possibilities. Its power is undeniable for it can easily dismiss our fears and begin to set our dreams in motion.

Moments of fear still came to visit me as I ventured forward into unknown territory. But I knew that I could not live in fear and from the heart at the same time. It is either one or the other. I wanted something to help me focus in those moments when fear was nudging my heart.

Something stopped me in front of the jewellery display case. A plain silver pendant on a chain with the engraved word, 'Faith', caught my attention. That was exactly what I needed! A reminder about faith. Faith was a new friend that I was still getting to know and only beginning to understand.

When we step out on the limb to follow our heart, we need to have faith. We need to have faith that life will provide and things will work out. We need to have faith in the wisdom of things we can't see. We need to trust that there is enough for all of us. We need to believe love will come to us at exactly the right time. We need to have faith in the power of our dreams.

I didn't know how I would learn to do all of that. I'd known my fears for so long. What I knew for sure was that I needed to simply follow my heart and that it was time to bring a little faith along for the ride.

2. I forgot to unplug myself from the electrical and water hook-up back at the campsite and I'm dragging the entire apparatus behind me, sending sparks flying in all directions.

3. I am pooping all over the road, creating dangerously slippery driving conditions behind me, seemingly oblivious to the fact that I forgot to put the cap back on the holding tank.

4. You detect the scent of burning muffins wafting through the air. This would mean that the muffins I'm baking are done and that I have also found the answer to the question about baking while driving.

~

It was not only along the road where *Miss Daisy* seemed to attract attention. One day my arrival at the campsite stopped a conversation dead in its tracks. Four women at the adjacent site turned their heads in curious unison as the expression on their faces read, "What the daisy is that?"

Once I had settled in and put up my dazzling new awning (these are the things that suddenly thrilled me in my little RV world) I decided to do a few exercises. Conversation was still on pause at the neighbouring site as I pulled out my yoga mat, resistance bands and stability ball, and began to do a few leg squats against the side of my RV. Out of the corner of my eye, I could see the four women watching me attentively. "What in the daisy is she doing now?"

I was in the middle of squat #10 when my next-door neighbour poked her head out of her window and said hello.

"I've been camped here for two weeks and you're the first person I've seen here doing any sort of exercise," she chortled.

I was certainly the oddball at this conformist campground. *Have I landed in the middle of the set of Desperate RV Housewives?* Besides my neighbour, not one other person spoke with me during the two nights I spent camped there.

"That's a weird trailer," I overheard two children say as they walked by *Miss Daisy* one afternoon. Considering that every other trailer in the park was basic white I guess I couldn't argue that point. No, this was not the type of RV park that celebrated RV diversity. I'd have to save my plans for an RV Pride Day for another park, another day.

I had suddenly found myself as the centre of attention and it was fine. *I'm okay with being different. I'm okay with being the one that stands out. I'm okay whether people like it or they don't. Frankly, I don't give a daisy.*

When you're just like everybody else, you're offering nothing more than your own conformity to the world. Our differences, our uniqueness, our creativity, our individual take on life - these are the unique gifts that we can offer instead.

There were many times when I quietly conformed and went unnoticed. It wasn't my intention to be deliberately non-conformist by becoming a Daisymobile driver. When I didn't follow in the footsteps of my older brother and sister and attend the same university as the rest of the gene pool, well, that was deliberately non-conformist.

Driving a Daisymobile was simply what I needed and wanted to do. I was just being me. But if I am remembered for having spent a summer driving *Miss Daisy*, living outside the proverbial box, encouraging others to live and look at life a little differently, that is perfectly all right by me.

And if there were a few more people exercising at RV campsites, I'd be fine with that too.

chapter 15

Larry, the Non-Conformist Cow

Manitoulin Island was calling my name and with good reason. It's not every day that you have the chance to meet an inspirational cow.

A visit to Manitoulin Island was not in my original plans but my plans changed after my stay at the conformist campground. Manitoulin Island, the world's largest freshwater island, lies in Lake Huron and is known as a jewel of Northern Ontario. I packed up *Miss Daisy*, bid farewell to my sedentary campsite neighbours and drove to a town called Little Current, the northernmost access town on Manitoulin. From there, I hopped on my bicycle, *Miss Daisy Too,* and headed off for a two-wheeled island adventure.

Manitoulin Island has a rich and diverse history. Apparently, the island was first occupied by Aboriginals over 9,000 years ago. Europeans and Jesuit missionaries arrived in the mid-1600s adding to the cultural depth and history of the island. Manitoulin is now home to several native tribes for whom the island holds a special power. Amongst the Aboriginals, 'Manitoulin' means 'home of the Great Spirit'.

I felt that 'spirit' wherever I went: from the peaceful serenity on the roads to the quaint farmer's fields and cottages that dotted the landscape to views of the rugged shoreline. It was easy to get lost in meditative thought. A few kilometres of cycling brought me to a small village where I saw a sign advertising a local artisan shop. I smiled, realizing why life had brought me to Manitoulin. I'd wanted a dream catcher to place inside *Miss Daisy*. What better place to find one than in the home of the Ojibwa?

The Ojibwa, also known as the 'Faith Keepers', are one of three tribes on Manitoulin. Who could be more qualified to help me keep my dreams and guard my faith? The Ojibwa believe that dreams have magical qualities such as the ability to change or direct your path in life. The dream catcher, a woven, webbed circle with a hole in the centre, captures dreams as they float by. The good dreams slip through the centre of the circle; the bad dreams become entangled in the webbing and perish in the light of day.

I hoped a dream catcher would help me hang on to my dreams, and help filter the good energy from the bad. *Maybe my Ojibwa dream catcher would also help me keep the faith, in those times when it may wane?* In looking to create the life of my dreams, I certainly wasn't averse to asking for a hand from the mystical side. When you wish to live life from the heart, you need to believe in things that you cannot see.

That night I hung my dream catcher in *Miss Daisy* and that night I had a vividly bad dream. It was the first bad dream that I'd had in some time. When I awoke the next morning, I reflected on the dream, finding it easy to let go of the fears that had visited in the night. It was as if they'd perished already, caught up in the web of my dream catcher.

All was good. I was already batting a thousand with my dream catcher.

~

There might have been another reason for me to visit Manitoulin. I serendipitously ran into a very inspirational cow. Allow me to explain.

While cycling one of the quiet back roads, past beautiful farm fields, I came across a field of cattle. There were 100 or so bovine eyes staring back at me in my brightly coloured cycling garb. I was a curious sight from their perspective I imagine. One of the cows, however, was not like the others.

Most of the herd was grazing on the farm side of the fence, following traditional cattle norms. One cow (that I had named Larry) jumped the fence and was wandering as freely along the road as I was with my bicycle. I was impressed by Larry and his get-up-and-go. Cattle are normally such conformist animals, living in herds, inside the fence, as cows are taught to do. They're not unlike us humans I suppose. But here was Larry, making a courageous leap into non-conformity and leaving behind the familiarity of his farm and friends he'd known all his life.

When I last saw Larry, he was heading down the road towards new and exciting pastures. He was moo-ving on you could say. (Sorry, I just couldn't resist!) After my recent experience in the conformist campground, he was an inspiration, a reminder to be true to myself, to embrace differences and to keep moo-ving on towards my dreams. As I watched his rump fade in the distance, I waved goodbye and shouted after him, "Larry, don't forget to stop at the artisan shop and pick up a dream catcher on your way out of town!"

chapter 16

Meeting the Spunky Women of Wawa

If I ever have a town of my own, I'm going to erect a giant wild daisy at the city limits to welcome visitors as they arrive. Canada has no shortage of towns that host Big Monuments of all sorts in an attempt to leave their imprint on the world. From Big Nickels to Flying Saucers to Giant Moose, Canada offers it all for the tourist in search of Big Things.

Wawa, Ontario offers visitors the Big Goose, a giant goose monument that welcomes visitors on their way into town. Many folks had suggested that I make the requisite two-minute stop at the Goose, grab a coffee at the local Tim Horton's and keep driving. Undaunted, I didn't feel that I'd cook my goose with a longer stay in Wawa, so I daringly booked myself in for two nights at the nearby campsite.

I awoke on the first morning and cycled into Goose town on my bicycle *Miss Daisy Too*. The Main Street was a typical small town, a one-stoplight affair. It was what I noticed out front of the pharmacy that told me that this was not just a small town with a big goose.

Back in Ottawa, I'd often seen folks, mainly seniors, making their way about town on four-wheeled scooters. But I'd never seen one like this before. This scooter sported a flashy blue "cab" on top, making it look like a very fun albeit very slow-moving car.

I stopped for a closer look and approached the grey-haired driver, Eileen, asking if I could take a photo.

"Sure! Why? Are you in the market for one?" she quipped. *Do I look like I am?*

"Hopefully not for a few years yet," I replied. *As in 30 or 40 or perhaps even 50 more years.*

Eileen told me that she couldn't go around town without getting noticed in her bright blue Shoprider. *Eileen, you spunky old bird, you're more noteworthy than the town big bird. In fact, you could likely attract even more tourists than the Big Goose so I'm not surprised.* Anyways, as a Daisymobile driver, I understood what she meant. Eileen stood out in the small crowd of Wawa.

Given the choice between "the usual scooter that everyone buys" or "the drive-me-if-you-dare Shoprider," Eileen opted to turn a few heads by not being ordinary. For her 80-plus years, Eileen was a big inspiration to anyone daring to live outside the box. Just a suggestion Wawa, but maybe it's time to put a giant Shoprider on the edge of town too?

~

As it turned out, Wawa is home to a number of inspirational women. Large wooden doors painted and decorated with images of older women were sprinkled throughout town, lining the sidewalks and the perimeter of the tourist centre. They were part of the 'Granny Doors' project, a way for local family members and friends to pay tribute to the women who'd influenced their lives and the town of Wawa.

Each door featured a character painting and tribute to a local woman, most often created by family members. The tributes included some interesting personal history and fun tidbits such as: "Mary is well-known for her lemon cake." Judging by the glass of wine in her hand, it seemed that Mary enjoyed more than just a piece of lemon cake.

There was a tribute to Marcia Anastasia Christoforides, also known as Lady Dunn. She was one of the largest female philanthropists in Canadian history, donating the equivalent of $300 million (in today's value) to various charitable causes. A highly independent and intelligent woman, she was noteworthy in life for a number of reasons, including her inclination for millionaires. She married two of them in her lifetime, both of whom were more than 30 years her senior. That they both predeceased her and she ended up a multi-millionaire is just a random coincidence I'm sure.

While she didn't marry a millionaire, Doetje Dykstra Stuiverkig or Dorothy as she was more commonly known, made her mark by being known as the 'Granny on the Bicycle'. Dorothy was from Holland and corresponded as a pen pal with a Wawa fellow by the name of

Marinus for a year and a half before they decided to take a chance on their relationship. That was back in the early 1950s, long before the Internet, good long-distance phone service, Skype, or any other modern-day advantages in courtship. She came to Canada on a ship from Holland, suffering from seasickness the entire voyage, to meet Marinus.

Dorothy took the risk to leave her familiar home, for one where she didn't speak the language, to meet a fellow she only knew through letters. She'd even arrived in Wawa long before the Big Goose was built! Dorothy was simply willing to take a big leap and see what would happen. Dorothy and Marinus married in 1954 and happily raised four children and 10 grandchildren, with whom she shared her love of cycling. She had simply followed her heart and, as a result, the wheels of life had turned in Dorothy's favour.

~

Wawa had much more to offer than just a big goose. Having met Eileen and read about these trail-blazing women who'd gone before me, I felt connected to a sisterhood of some sort. These women of Wawa were willing to go against the grain and take large leaps of faith. And their lives, by example, seemed to demonstrate that it was worthwhile to do so.

It was calming to meet these Wawa women as I ventured forward into much change of my own. I felt thankful to look to those who had leapt before me, for a nod of encouragement. As I waved goodbye to Wawa, I am fairly certain that I heard Eileen, Mary, Lady Dunn, Dorothy and the rest of the Wawa women say, "Go for it, Heather, you'll be fine." I think I also heard the Big Goose offer me a few words of advice too. "Follow your heart Heather, don't follow my example. I'm headed south this winter."

chapter 17

Where's a Sign
When You Need One?

I had a ritual that I practiced nightly before bed. I always wrote some words of thanks in my gratitude journal. Then I browsed through my 'dream book', a collection of photos and words that reflected my goals and dreams. Lastly, I had a talk with the universe, asking for guidance or seeking an answer to a question. It had been a quiet few days and I was feeling restless, unsure as to which direction life was sending me. The Protestant work ethic within me was slightly worried that I wasn't moving forward quickly enough to wherever I thought I needed to be.

One night I frankly asked the universe to send me a sign as to where to go or what to do next? *Please God, anyone up there, send me a sign, some sort of sign.* And then I went to sleep, confident that someone had heard me or that, at the very least, my message had been left on some sort of cosmic answering machine.

The next day, my plan was to cycle into Thunder Bay to see the sights. The helpful clerk (Yes! Another nice, non-axe murderer whom I'd met on my travels. Life is good!) at the Info Centre highly recommended seeing the Mount McKay Lookout, which, she said, offered a stunning panoramic view of Thunder Bay and its environs.

I heeded her suggestion and headed off on *Miss Daisy Too* to find Mount McKay.

I came across a 'sign' rather quickly although it wasn't exactly the kind of sign I'd been hoping for. The first sign that I encountered, just a few kilometres from my campsite, was a collection of 40 or 50 signs pointing in all directions to major cities around the world, noting the travel distance to each. *I asked for a sign telling me where to go next and you send me a sign that goes in all directions! Do they send you to comedy school before you can get a job at Magical Dream Place Headquarters?* Life's sense of humour and lack of direction would foreshadow the events for the remainder of my day.

The Bluffs Scenic Lookout would be my first stop. From its location on the city map, the lookout seemed to promise a wonderful view of the city, harbour and Lake Superior. I cycled in the vicinity of the lookout, looking for signs pointing me in the right direction. Do you sense a recurring theme yet? None were to be found. A few mistaken turns later and by the power of my own sleuthing skills, I finally found my own way to the Bluffs Lookout a few minutes later.

Thank goodness for my sense of direction but some signs would have been nice. I even glanced around for any signs of a camera crew. *Am I on Candid Camera right now?*

Mount McKay, which stands 1,000 feet above Thunder Bay, beckoned in the distance so I quickly ate lunch and headed off in its direction.

I still naively hoped to see some signs pointing me in the right direction even though all the signs I'd received so far indicated that there would be no signs. Indeed, I did not see one Mount McKay sign, so I simply kept cycling in the direction of the large knoll in the distance, like a pilgrim venturing across the desert towards the Pyramids. *Surely there will be signs as I get closer. What tourist attraction doesn't have signs to help people find their way?*

The evidence would suggest that Mount McKay doesn't.

I turned here and then I turned there, appearing to get closer to my destination. My frustration began to increase exponentially however, when I began to circumnavigate the lookout on a road that wound around its base. *Arrgh.* I could see the lookout, but I couldn't find the road that would lead me from here to there.

Finally, a well-worn sign appeared, slightly hidden by foliage. It read, and how I wish I was kidding here: "If you miss Mount McKay, you've missed Thunder Bay." In smaller print at the bottom of the sign read "Mount McKay, next right." *You put up ONE sign to direct people to Mount McKay and you put it here?* I would not be surprised to learn that people have died, gotten divorced or been led away in a straight jacket in the pursuit of trying to find Mount McKay. Mount Needle-in-a-Haystack would be a far more appropriate name for this reclusive mound.

If Mount McKay hadn't teased me enough that day, I still had a steep four km uphill climb to get to the lookout. *Mount McKay you sure know how to show a girl a good time, don't you?*

~

"You made it all the way up here on your bicycle?" one of the women said as she stepped out of her car at the top. It wasn't the climb that nearly killed me, it was the lack of signage.

The woman in the car was from Winnipeg and was travelling with two of her friends. Finally surrounded by the panoramic view of Lake Superior, the Sleeping Giant and Thunder Bay, we enjoyed a group laugh about the lack of signage en route to Mount McKay and marvelled that we'd arrived at all. I mentioned that my next stop was Winnipeg where I was headed to participate in a charity bike ride.

"Where are you staying while in Winnipeg?" one of them asked.

"I don't know yet, I don't plan that far ahead," I replied.

"What route will the charity bike ride be following?" was the next question.

"I don't know but they give out maps."

"Do you have a GPS?" she asked.

"Uh, no."

"Well, I guess you're just going to find your way" she said.

Bingo. A light bulb went on above my head. *Yes, I'm just going to find my way.* That was precisely the message that I needed to hear.

Duh! In my moment of discomfort, I'd been asking for a sign when, in fact, I didn't need one at all. Life had guided me in its usual humorous fashion by offering me either a plethora of signs or no signs at all. *Heather, you choose where you want to go or Heather, you figure out the next move.*

When you're in tune with your heart, you don't need a sign. You intuitively know that where you are is exactly where you're meant to be. Signs will only present themselves, to nudge you just a little bit, when they're absolutely needed, as they did at the final turnoff to Mount McKay. I'd temporarily forgotten this simple truth and life had a bit of fun reminding me of it that day.

I didn't mind their fun pranks. The folks at the Magical Dream Place Headquarters had my best interests at heart and they always left a smile on my face. They certainly did that day as I cycled past a beautiful display of wild daisies that adorned the roadside on the way back down from the lookout. *Yes, I'll find my way. But it's nice to see some wild daisies from time to time letting me know that I'm headed in the right direction. Thanks for the 'sign' guys!*

chapter 18

Death on Board
Miss Daisy

I will be anything but contrite here. I was happy that there'd finally been a death on board *Miss Daisy*.

I had left Thunder Bay that afternoon, driving west towards a tiny town called Wabigoon. This stretch of the drive took me along a fairly remote section of the Trans-Canada in Northern Ontario that is most known for, well, being remote. The most predominant signs of life are in the many trees that line the roadside as well as the occasional bear you might see out hunting for blueberries.

I continued on my way eventually arriving at the most nondescript of campsites in Wabigoon, beautifully situated adjacent to the hum of the traffic along the TransCanada. If you're seeking a romantic getaway for yourself and your special someone this would not be the place.

There didn't seem to be an overload of options in terms of recreational activities at the campsite either. When the campsite owner hopped into her golf cart to show me to my site, I got rather excited.

"Cool, I get to ride in this?"

"No," she said, "Just follow me in your RV."

My singular moment of opportune fun had quickly come and gone.

I got *Miss Daisy* comfortably settled in for the night. With no other form of recreation to get me into trouble, I pulled out my equipment to do a few exercises. The previous week I'd added a bit more air to my stability ball, which now meant it wasn't as svelte as it used to be and required a bit more wrestling to get it out the door of *Miss Daisy*. I gave it an extra push out the door and left it outside while I retrieved a few other items.

It was then that it happened. The ball was lying adjacent to the door. I pushed the door open a bit further when the pointy corner of the door made contact with the now firmly inflated ball. Kaboom! Death came quickly. The ball was gone.

I looked at its limp, airless body and didn't feel any remorse for my role in its demise. The ball had begun to get on my nerves recently. It took up excess space in *Miss Daisy*, it rolled around at will as I drove and it was awkward to push it out of the door. It had become the classic unwanted houseguest. At least it hadn't been nibbling on my private stash of chocolate-covered almonds.

I didn't intentionally kill the ball. I didn't take a knife to it in a moment of frustration. I had however begun to think that I didn't really want the ball around anymore. *Be careful what you wish for.*

I'd spent the past few months simplifying and decluttering my life, my living space and my mind. I'd spent time and energy creating intention in my RV using feng shui. Why the heck was I driving around with a big red ball that was taking up more than its fair share of my small space and niggling on my mind?

It was an act of divine intervention. A helpful reminder from the universe to continue to ask some key questions: *Why am I keeping this? Why am I bringing this along? How is this serving me?* And the biggie of all questions, do I love it enthusiastically? I didn't mind the space that my bicycle, *Miss Daisy Too*, occupied inside the RV, but that ball.... I wasn't having a ball with the ball anymore.

~

The sudden death of the ball had another unforeseen advantage. It certainly livened up my stay at the Wabigoon campground that night. I didn't want my neighbours, who likely heard the explosion, suspecting a crime of any sort. If they were going to point a finger at anyone for any sort of crime, I just knew it'd be me, the oddball, the Daisymobile driver. It had merely been an accident. Nonetheless, I meticulously cleaned up any potentially suspicious evidence, hid the remains in a secret location and quietly sat around my campsite reading People magazine like a normal RVer.

Deep inside, I was happy about the death of the ball. I think that *Miss Daisy* was relieved as well. After all, she had lent a helping door to the ball's deathly fate. I can't help but wonder if she wanted the ball out of her life too.

We continued on our journey enjoying the newfound freedom and spaciousness on board *Miss Daisy*. When one door closes, a window of opportunity opens. Or, in this case, when one door opens, a ball explodes. It's the same thing.

chapter 19

A Tall RV Meets a Low Bridge and Everyone Lives Happily Ever After

When you're travelling solo, there will eventually come a time when you'll find out whether you truly accept yourself: the good, the bad and the stupid. Life will either hit you in the head with an epiphany of some sort or it'll hit you in the air conditioner. In my case, it was the latter.

As I began to plan my trip, I did wonder whether I'd get bored, lonely, tired of myself or heaven forbid, discover that I didn't even like myself. I'd always travelled with friends or family. Either I hadn't felt confident enough to travel by myself or I was afraid of being by myself for too long. There'd be no one to blame when I got lost, no one else to keep me entertained and no one to lean on when things went awry. But then again, I'd have my stash of chocolate-covered almonds all to myself.

By the time I'd reached Winnipeg, I'd happily discovered that I felt quite comfortable with myself and was in fact able to have fun on my own. Okay, squirt-gun fights were a bit of a challenge, but all other options for fun were fair game. It was in Winnipeg, however, that I learned a rather crushing lesson about the importance of loving myself even in my less than shining moments.

~

Yep, I did it. I committed a classic RV blunder.

I was leaving the Winnipeg Zoo when I came upon a bridge that wasn't marked for height. Should you ever decide to embark upon the RV lifestyle it's rather useful if not imperative to know the exact height of your particular RV. Measure the height of your RV folks. Not that I followed this piece of my own advice I might add. I overlooked that fairly major trip preparation detail back in the days when I was busy adding the right feng shui touches to my RV world. Anyways, it's against good judgement, as my story will demonstrate, to venture under a low-hanging, unmarked bridge.

As I approached the bridge, I was feeling as positive as a rear-view mirror, optimistically thinking that "objects may be larger than they appear." The height of the bridge looked 'about' right but again, a word of caution here, when you're talking about thousands of dollars of equipment potentially hitting concrete, it's nice to know some details.

My better judgement took one look at what was happening and fled the scene. I continued to inch forward towards the bridge. As I eyed the entrance to the bridge, I crouched down in the driver's seat, apparently hopeful that would make some sort of a difference to the overall height of my vehicle. Any optometrists in the crowd would have suspected that I was suffering from some serious depth perception issues.

Positive thinking did me absolutely no good that day. As I made my way under the bridge the next sound I heard was not a round of applause from a cheering crowd: "Wow Heather, good eye on the bridge!" Instead, I was greeted by the rather horrific smacking sound of my rooftop air-conditioning unit French-kissing the bridge. Uh oh.

~

In the past, I'd generally been able to conceal my moments of stupidity or poor judgement. There were be no such hope as I reversed my large, daisy-covered butt out from under the bridge in front of roughly 50 pairs of eyes. *Dear God, just this once, may no one notice the daisies or the website address on the side of my RV. Maybe I should change the slogan on the side of Miss Daisy? "Follow your heart, wherever it takes you. Caution: Some restrictions, including low bridges, may apply."*

We all have those moments when we do not shine our brightest, moments that we wish hadn't happen, or moments that we hope others didn't notice. As I looked around, there was no one but myself to look at for responsibility. I allowed myself a brief pity party, but quickly realized I still had a long road ahead, travelling with myself. Sooner would be a better time than later to focus on loving myself through times such as this.

I gave myself some slack. I was still adjusting to my new RV life. I recalled the salsa I had purchased before I arrived in Winnipeg. Space is an issue when you live in an RV, a small fact that I overlooked when I purchased a jar of salsa the size of an infant. I hadn't wondered as to how or where I'd store it. I ended up with salsa that wouldn't fit in the fridge and later, an RV that got stuck under a bridge. Somehow, I had landed myself smack in the middle of a Dr. Seuss book about RVing.

~

Upon arriving at the RV service centre to have my air conditioner replaced, I briefly entertained the thought of trying to hide my blunder.

"It was the craziest thing. I was just driving along when this meteorite, mysteriously shaped like a daisy, came out of nowhere and crashed into my roof...." I wondered whether they'd likely heard that story before so I opted for the truth instead.

My momentary lapse of judgment cost me $1,108.69. Even at that price, it was a speck of dust in an adventure that had already yielded so much more. Our mistakes, blunders, less-than-glamorous moments are always small specks in a much grander scheme of our bigger and more spectacular lives.

Is there such a thing as a mistake anyway? That week was unusually hot and as I relaxed at my campsite the following evening, enjoying the benefits of my brand new, fully functioning air-conditioning unit, I pondered that thought. It may have been the best thing that happened to me that week.

A refreshing chill went up my spine as I relaxed in the coolness. I liked myself. I loved myself. I was even able to laugh at myself. No matter what I might do. And that was darned good stuff to know.

chapter 20

Prairie Possibilities

I love pancakes. Maybe that's why I enjoyed the prairies so much.

"You'll be bored out of your mind, it's as flat as a pancake out there," many folks had said about crossing the prairies between Manitoba and Alberta. "There's nothing to see so just keep on driving."

The beauty of a pancake is in the eye of the diner though, isn't it? The truth is that the prairies are really more like a waffle, there are a few dips and valleys here and there. My apologies, I tend to digress when the topic of anything carbohydrate comes up.

The prairie landscape greeted me with open roads, endless vistas of farm fields and a breathtaking panoramic view of the horizon. Surprisingly, I found the contrast from where I'd begun to be quite beautiful.

We live in a world in which we're surrounded by things and stuff. How often do we truly get to enjoy an uncluttered view of the world without buildings or bridges getting in the way? How often do we truly get to enjoy an uncluttered view of our own self without our thoughts, beliefs or self-imposed limits getting in our way?

This is what the prairies offered. After having extricated myself from a busy city-dwelling life filled with stuff, the prairies prodded my thinking in a refreshing new way. They represented an expansiveness of possibilities, a place without limits or boundaries and a place where my heart could wander freely. The prairies called my name. *What's next Heather? What do you want to see on the landscape ahead of you?*

I'd just left behind the life that I no longer loved. I'd been doing things that no longer filled me with joy. I had been surrounded by buildings and a cityscape that no longer nurtured my heart and soul. The life that I had surrounded myself with had, quite literally, emotionally and spiritually obscured my perspective on myself and on my life. I wasn't about see what else might be possible.

The prairies are beautifully uncluttered. Against the backdrop of seemingly endless horizon and open sky is a place where dreams and possibilities can unfold and expand. Compared to the mindless bustle of city life, the prairies achieve their effect with subtlety and the quiet power of natural suggestion. Effortlessly, I found my thoughts and my vision flowing far beyond my normal horizon. I'll admit that, on occasion, my thoughts did drift back to pancakes ... with blueberries ... and maple syrup. Heck, I couldn't keep my monkey mind on self-development stuff all day long.

I felt cleansed as I crossed the prairies. It'd seemed that some more of the limits I'd put on myself and my life vanished with each setting sun. I relished in the simplified landscape and my simplified life. I savoured the open view on the road ahead.

The prairies had done their job. New possibilities had indeed begun to appear on my own horizon. My plans for the fall were about to change.

chapter 21

Just Say Yes!

"Let's just say yes to everything!" we all hollered enthusiastically. Random acts of enthusiasm are often how these sorts of adventures begin.

I'd only known Pat and Tara for a couple of days at that point. We'd met on a Caribbean cruise in October 2008 and had become friends faster than you can say daisy, spending most of our free time together.

On that particular day, we were discussing the fact that we'd all said 'yes' to the last-minute irresistible offer from our friend Peggy to join her on the cruise. We also discussed the fact that we could have easily found a long list of reasons to say 'no' to her offer.

How often do we say 'no' to ourselves in a day? How often do we say 'no' to what we really want? How often do we say 'no' to what is possible? No, I can't do that. No, I can't afford that. No, I am not fit enough. No, I don't have the time. No, I can't have cake. No, "insert your reason here."

No doesn't feel good. It limits us. Yes feels great! It allows us.

Saying yes is like taking your life out of the realm of ordinary and putting whipped cream, a cherry and chocolate sauce on top.

Tara, Pat and I decided that for one day we would just say 'yes' to whatever life presented. Within legal, moral and ethical boundaries, of course, we agreed to say yes to it all. Drinks, dessert, excursions, staying up late, dancing, shopping, new shoes, new people, we gave everything the green 'yes' light.

It was awesome. It was transformative. It was liberating. It changed our day. Yes. It changed our lives.

It certainly had a dramatic effect on mine.

~

The three of us met up again in Calgary, after I'd arrived there with *Miss Daisy*. On our first road trip to a place called the Badlands, conversation quickly turned to how our lives had evolved since our synchronous meeting on the cruise, all because of the word 'yes'.

In those six months, I'd said yes to the sale of my house. I'd said yes to simplifying my life. I'd said yes to my dream of adventuring across Canada. I'd said yes to trying something completely new. I'd finally said yes to what I truly wanted to do in life. Most importantly, I had finally said yes to my inner voice. I'd begun to learn that if I wished to be true to myself and to follow my heart, I needed to say 'yes' when it came calling.

I was paying close attention to my heart at the time. I had felt another 'yes' on the horizon as I'd crossed the prairies. It must have been the influence of the prairie perspective because I began to see other possibilities in my future.

~

My plan to follow my heart wherever it took me was proceeding very well, in exact accordance with the loose plan that such a heart-centered plan requires. It was my original plan to head to Vancouver Island by September and return to Ottawa in October that had begun to feel out-of-sync.

Playful thoughts of staying on the West Coast for the winter began to surface as I crossed the prairies, staring daily into the open expanse on the horizon. I hadn't wined and dined on that possibility before.

It's interesting when the pinging of new possibilities begin to surface in our hearts, isn't it? They speak to us quietly, in soft whispers of: "Hey, you could do this?" or "Have you thought of that?" Our brain then pipes in with its discouraging thoughts. "You can't do that, You shouldn't do that" or "You're crazy to try that." It's like Yes versus No in a tennis match, each volleying the ball of decision back and forth, until a winner is eventually declared.

I heard the soft whispers as I crossed the prairies, after nearly a month on the road. "You could stay out west for the winter. It would be warm enough to live in your RV." I heard the other voices too. "But what will people say? What will they think? When are you going to buy a house? Where are you going to work?" I stood on the sidelines as Yes battled No, well aware that there would be only one winner at the end of the match.

~

Here's a good piece of advice that I have learned from, surprisingly, my own advice. When you're in need of some advice, you may already be in possession of the best advice you could find, which is your own. I certainly was.

If you're asking the question, if you have the thoughts, then you already know the answer to your question. That was the advice I'd offered a friend only a few days earlier. She was in the midst of trying to make an important decision and asked what she thought I should do.

When I was seeking to make an important decision of my own a few days later, that piece of advice flew back at me like a boomerang. I'd had my thoughts too. The only question that remained was whether I would allow myself to say another yes. *Duh. Follow your heart, wherever it takes you.* My heart was asking me to stay on the Island for the winter. I just couldn't let it down since it'd brought me that far already. As I gazed ahead at the fork in the road, a yes crossed my lips. Excited, *Miss Daisy* and I then turned onto the road less travelled to see where it would lead.

Then I wondered if I dared to ask my Mom to knit a sweater to help keep *Miss Daisy* warm over the winter.

chapter 22

chapter 23

Thoughts From On Top of a Glacier

A trip up the Athabasca Glacier on the Columbia Icefield in the Canadian Rockies would be the first tourist excursion I'd taken since leaving Niagara Falls. I tended to explore places on my own, away from hoards of tourists, preferring to let my meanderings unfold in a more organic fashion. After 40-plus years of following the herd, I preferred experiencing life and the locales on my own terms.

I hadn't originally intended upon going to Jasper (note that change in plans is starting to become a recurring theme here!), a quaint mountain town that sits at the north end of the Columbia Icefield Parkway. After doing some research on the area, I changed my mind, deciding that I would enjoy a visit to the Athabasca Glacier. Or rather, it was likely my heart telling me that it wanted to go to the glacier for some reason.

The drive along the Icefields Parkway is rated one of the most scenic drives in the world. I wouldn't dispute that fact. The drive is magnificently surreal in its beauty. At every turn I was open-mouthed awed by the Rockies. *What kind of power creates such a place?*

The Athabasca Glacier sits at the mid-point of the Parkway, halfway between Banff and Jasper. Visitors to the six-kilometre long glacier are transported onto the glacier by snow bus. It was a steep drive up in some sections, like being taken up the side of a sno-cone. Our driver, Dave, deposited us safely at the top and we were left on our own to explore the glacier. Like the other tourists, I took the requisite photos and drank some of the glacial water. Then I sought a quieter spot from which to savour my awe-full glacier experience.

As I savoured the beauty that surrounded me, all I could do was thank the universe for guiding me there. Something changed in me as I glanced around at the icy magnitude before me, appreciating the life forces that had converged to create such a divine place. Something changed as I looked around and experienced LIFE on a much grander scale than I'd ever seen before. I don't know what force acted upon me that day, but suddenly I felt the clarity and motivation to make a big decision. I made a big commitment to myself and my dreams.

~

"Dream big!" Tony had said, during one of the energy healing sessions I'd had before leaving Ottawa. We were discussing my career direction and aspirations that day. I'd felt intimidated by his comments. I was afraid to have big dreams. I was afraid of failing. I didn't feel confident about my ability to achieve those dreams, I just didn't know how to make them happen. I didn't truly believe in my own larger-scale possibilities. But back then, I hadn't stood upon a glacier!

I couldn't be amidst such beauty and grandeur and not believe in the possibilities of life. If it was possible for the earth's forces to create such magnificence, then I had to ask myself, *What is possible for me?* In that moment, I felt possibility on a grand scale.

I'd lived small long enough. It was time for me to start thinking and dreaming bigger. The pounding in my heart told me that it liked the thoughts of bigger possibilities too.

What do you really want for yourself in life, Heather? The answers on the glacier were clear and honest. I want to write a book about my experiences of following my heart. I want to become a successful, published author and I want to help others with my story.

I have a message to share and I enjoy public speaking. I want to become one of North America's top inspirational speakers.

I want to marry my soul mate.

I want to live in my dream home.

I want to live the life of my dreams, a life that I Love.

I'd given much thought to all of these possibilities as I made my way across Canada. I'd also dismissed them all in rather short order as not possible. They had seemed rather lofty wishes. Keeping my wishes small had kept my fears quiet and my dreams within range. My time on the glacier gave me no choice but to think of my life on

we've ended up driving our RV on the wrong side of the road."

Me: My inside voice, beginning to get concerned, was encouraging me to ask which direction they were headed in. *Heather, you want to be driving 'with' the Australians, not 'against' them.* Instead, I just nodded.

Aussie again: "And we ain't seen much wildlife either. We haven't seen a thing since we've been here."

Me: "That's too bad." *Well I can imagine why! Word has spread throughout the wildlife population about the RV-driving Aussies. Once a whiff of their accent hits town all the elk, deer, sheep and the rest of the gang hightail it for the hills. 'Bob, Fred, the Australians are back. It's time to pack up the women and children and get out of here. They're weaving all over the road, deliriously melting in their polar fleeces while out in search of fall foliage, snow and running maple syrup. It's not safe for us out there right now.'*

My laundry finished and I bid farewell to the Australians. It had been fun to come into contact with them, within the confines of the laundromat of course.

chapter 25

The One True Love

Spending day after day on the road by myself afforded me much time to ponder a miscellany of things. *Where should I head to next? When will I finish that damn jar of salsa? I wonder what ever happened to Larry the Cow?*

Some days I pondered larger issues like The One True Love.

I had just finished a phone conversation with my friend Pat who mentioned that she'd shared news of my travels with one of her friends of the male persuasion. This gentleman friend had told Pat that he couldn't believe a woman would spend the summer adventuring without some sort of travelling companion, i.e. man by her side. His exact words were "that it was impossible."

Hold on a moment, Pat. I looked around inside *Miss Daisy*. Nope, there was no one else there. I looked under *Miss Daisy*. Nope, there was no one else there either. I looked over both shoulders, around me and beside me. Nope, I didn't see anyone there either.

"Pat, tell him that it is indeed very possible. In fact, I'm doing it. Also tell him that it's not 1950 anymore and that women can vote now and everything."

Who says that we can't travel the road of life alone at times? Who says that we need a companion, male or female? Where does that belief come from? Sure, I have a few travelling companions with me: the Doobie Brothers, Cher, Madonna, Paul Simon and my Radar Jammin' Guardian Angel, but I don't need anyone else, friend or lover, tagging along this part of my life journey.

In fact, I wanted to be on my own. I wanted to travel alone so that I could finally find my One True Love.

~

I'm not talking about finding that One True Love in someone else. Society and most of the magazines at the grocery store checkout line suggest that we seek true love in someone else. They suggest that we need to travel through life with someone in order to be complete. Their concept is that once we find someone who will love us, then we'll have found our own happiness and fulfillment.

Well, I'd tried on those shoes before and they didn't seem to fit. I'd spent much time and effort trying to find love 'out there' somewhere only to discover that happiness still eluded me. Why? Wasn't that the equation? Me plus someone else equals happiness? Apparently it wasn't. This was my time to travel solo. This was my time to view life through a different lens, to try another way of creating love by starting with myself. *Heather, you need to begin here, inside of yourself. That's where you'll find your One True Love.* To find my ideal partner, first I needed to discover my ideal Me.

~

Cycling had become a form of meditation, one that I enjoyed regularly on my travels. It quieted my mind, filled my soul and offered me new perspectives on life as the kilometres rolled by. I thought about the One True Love that morning, on the 50-km ride up to Rogers Pass, one of British Columbia's most spectacular mountain crossings.

Solitude and aloneness can be an uneasy place for social beings like humans. The thought can be so uneasy for some as to be deemed 'impossible.' We don't like to be reminded of our own discomforts. A travelling companion in life may provide comfort, at least for a period of time. Yet ending our own solitude may only offer us the illusion of comfort when, in fact, we still have none. On our own, we're left to find how to fill our own lives and more critically, how to fill ourselves.

My trip was not always easy on my own, but it was far from impossible. I didn't mind life on my own. On the contrary, I actually preferred it that way. I began to cherish my aloneness as a precious and necessary commodity, one that I'd not enjoyed nearly enough over the past few years. The opportunity to create my days, my experiences and my life on my terms was a most welcome blessing. Truths are revealed in our quiet and alone moments. It was in those moments that I began to find my own answer about my One True Love.

The answer was quite simple. I had to begin by creating a loving relationship with myself. The process of getting there was the complicated part. It would involve an undertaking of enough life experiences to fill this book and roughly 57 more of the same size. Nonetheless, the solo Daisymobile driver adventure was a huge positive step in the right direction.

Rogers Pass is often called the 'Crown Jewel' of the TransCanada highway. The spectacular view of the craggy snow-capped mountains and smooth glaciers is stunning. I imagine that if you could bottle the feeling of The One True Love it would be similar to the feelings experienced admiring the grandeur atop Rogers Pass. It simply fills your heart and soul, all on its own.

I didn't need a travelling companion to give me that feeling. I didn't need a travelling companion to share the view. It was a feeling and a view that I was quite happy to reflect upon all on my own.

chapter 26

My Golden Luck

I'd always thought that Tina Turner should have released a song entitled, "What's Luck Got to Do With It?" given our societal preoccupation with the concept of luck.

I'd begun to think more about luck recently after a few friends had made comments suggesting that I was lucky to be able to embark on this solo adventure. Our human perception of luck, when it greets us in our own lives or in the lives of others, intrigued me.

I don't really believe in luck nor do I believe that I am any more or less lucky than the next person. I am grateful for what I have and I accept what life brings my way. I believe we create our lives and our experiences in a number of ways. And, of course, I believe in listening to and following my heart.

I felt inspired and shared some thoughts about luck on my Facebook wall that evening:

> Luck, whether good or bad, has nothing to do with it. We are where we are because of the choices we've made, the thoughts we've carried with us, the risks we've taken or not taken, and actions we've put into motion. That's the hard truth of life. We're the only ones that we can hold accountable for where

we are and how we respond when life offers us the good or the bad.

The next morning I awoke to learn that dramatic irony isn't just for Shakespearean plays, it could visit my life as well. In a startling twist of events, *Miss Daisy*'s usually reliable engine wouldn't start. I would have several hours to ponder thoughts on luck and to nibble on the words I'd written the night before.

~

I had intended to leave my campsite, which was situated about 50 km east of Rogers Pass, B.C., and head to Cranbrook for a few days. Due to its steep incline, tunnels, sharp curves and unpredictable shifts in weather, Rogers Pass is known to be a challenging drive. After doing some research online, I'd decided that I wasn't comfortable making the drive in *Miss Daisy*. Instead, I would drive to Cranbrook, which would mean a more circuitous route through the mountains, but one that felt more comfortable.

When life presents us with good or bad, often they are just the flip sides of the same coin. I try to accept that both have a role in our lives, for reasons that may not immediately be apparent. When *Miss Daisy* wouldn't start, instead of feeling panicked or frustrated, I simply wondered why this challenge was being presented to me. The answer would come soon enough.

~

Ted, the tow truck driver, arrived to prepare *Miss Daisy* to be taken to the town of Golden, about 23 km east of our campsite. I stood back and watched Ted work, appreciating the attentiveness and patience with which he handled my precious cargo. It was a good sign.

Our thoughts can run amuck at such times. *What's wrong with Miss Daisy? How much will the repair cost? How much time will it take? Will my giant jar of salsa survive the tow?* I grasped my faith pendant and looked up to the sky, seeking some guidance. *Do I need to be concerned about this situation?* My heart answered me in calmness, telling me not to worry. My stomach then piped in telling me to pick up some nacho chips to go with the salsa. I knew that we'd all be just fine.

If you ever need a tow in the vicinity of Golden, ask for Ted. He spent over an hour readying *Miss Daisy* for the tow, even summoning his wife from Golden to deliver extra bungee cords to secure the towing lights. I sensed that Ted was a special tow truck driver, he put such thought and care into his work. You don't want just anyone touching your daisies!

We chatted easily on the drive into town. Ted was a retired logger, who'd spent most of his life in Golden. He told me that he used to work at a nearby campground where he met travellers from around the world. On one occasion, he befriended a couple of Australians who'd told him that while in Canada they wanted to see a bear and a moose. *I wonder if it was the same couple I met back in the laundromat in Jasper? Were they hoping to see snow too?*

Ted drove the Aussies to the outskirts of town where they waited. In a matter of minutes, a moose appeared. The Australians were thrilled.

"Look in the rear view mirror," Ted then said. There was a black bear behind their vehicle. What kind of divine luck is that, I wonder?

Ted seemed like the type of guy who could bring wishes and people together. As I listened to him tell that story, I knew my wishes would be granted too; to get *Miss Daisy* fixed easily and inexpensively, and to be on my way to Cranbrook that same day.

~

Dark skies loomed as we pulled into the garage. Like a scene from emergency room television, *Miss Daisy* was wheeled into the shop within minutes and I headed to the waiting area. An hour or so later, *Miss Daisy* was miraculously fixed and ready to go. As I packed up my things and prepared to pay my bill, a frazzled-looking man rushed in the door, arriving at the service counter. I overheard him tell the clerk that he'd been driving his motor home down Rogers Pass when a heavy wind and rainstorm hit. A tree had fallen on his RV, which now needed extensive repairs.

There we were, him and I, two different travellers who'd made two different choices, who'd had two different experiences of 'luck' on the same day. I also got my wish. I'd been right about Ted. The repair to *Miss Daisy* was not overly expensive and I arrived safely in Cranbrook that evening. I only forgot one thing: I should have asked Ted to show me a moose and a bear too.

chapter 27

California Dreamin'

It started off sounding like a far-fetched idea that at some point didn't seem all that far-fetched anymore.

"Heather, when you get to Vancouver, just turn left and head to California!" was the advice of a fellow RVer I'd met who spends the winters in California. I initially laughed it off as a crazy idea but then began to think, *Well, I've made it this far in a Daisymobile, what's a bit further?* California was beginning to entice me.

It may have also been due to the fact that I'd shared one of my other California dreams with a few of my friends in recent days. I said that I wanted to be on the Ellen Show someday; for what, why, how or when, I didn't know. Most likely not my less than dazzling dance moves but for some sort of noteworthy talent. I only knew that it was a dream of mine even if it felt a bit remote at the time.

A conversation with my friend Tara cured me of that feeling quite quickly. Whenever I need to talk about possibilities and 'yes' living, Tara is my go-to gal. By the end of our phone call, I'd set a very clear intention that I was going to be on the *Ellen Show* someday, somehow. Tara had also coached me on a few things I could do to help manifest my dream. The decision was made. It was a big dream but one to which I said, *Why not me?*

"If I had to live life all over again, I'd pick more daisies," read the quote my friend had forwarded to me that same day. It had its origins with an 85-year-old woman as she looked back upon her life. I was doing quite fine in the daisy department, confident that a shortage of daisy-picking outings would not be one of my regrets in later years.

Nonetheless, I didn't want to look back upon my life one day with regrets of any sort. I didn't want to say that *I wish I'd done this or I wish I'd done that. I wish I'd tried to get on the Ellen Show. I wish I'd gone to California. I wish I'd finished that bag of Oreos.* I wanted to know that I'd done everything I could to have lived a life to the fullest and not left any of my dreams behind.

And that's how my *Ellen Show* dream began.

~

I like to add a few visuals or props to my bigger dreams to encourage their growth. I had purchased an *Ellen Show* coffee mug, but decided that I also needed a picture of Ellen for my dream book. I had not yet had luck procuring the latter item.

As I travelled, I noticed the subtle and sometimes not-so subtle nuances of a place that either lifted my energy and spirit or did not. My heart was a wonderful gauge, quickly letting me know whether there was harmony between my self, my environment and my surroundings. The message was loud and clear in this particular town. *Heather, Leave.* After only one night, I felt uneasy there and decided to heed the suggestion of my heart.

I hit the Walmart for a few snacks and groceries before leaving town. The cover of *Oprah* magazine caught my attention out of the corner of my eye so I added the daytime diva's magazine to my items. *Miss Daisy* and I were on the road again, and I trusted that my heart would find us a more pleasing place to stay for our next stopover.

It was the first time on my trip that I did not have a destination in mind for the end of the day. My only criteria was to find a place that felt good. I drove for several hours, passing a few towns on our way, none of which had grabbed my attention. I could hear my heart saying to me at each town, *No Heather, this isn't it. Keep driving.*

When it feels right, you just know it. You may not know why it's right at the time, just accept that it is.

I'd just left behind the last of the major towns along the highway out of Kamloops and was headed into the more remote hills of the Canadian desert, just past the Okanagan Valley. I felt a noticeable shift in my own energy as each corner in the road welcomed me with another stunning view of mystical desert terrain. My heart lifted and a chord of music was struck within my soul. This was where I needed to be.

"Savona 13 km," read the sign along the highway. *What a soothing sounding name for a town.* It was getting later into the afternoon and I wanted to set up camp soon. I made a wish to the universal RV campsite powers that be: *Find me a quiet, affordable campsite with a great view, along this stretch of highway.* I only wish that all of my wishes could be granted so quickly. Two kilometres later, just past Savona, I found campsite heaven on earth. It was peaceful, quiet and adjacent to the lake, the most wonderful and least expensive campsite I'd enjoyed all summer. The message from my heart that day was loud and clear. *Thanks life, this place rocks.*

I can't fully explain how life works at times, but I have to marvel at its brilliance after days such as that. It only seemed fitting to finish the day by hanging out with one of my favourite celebrities, Oprah.

 I always appreciate the insights and wisdom she shares. A passage that I came across in her magazine that evening seemed written for me and where I was in that moment in my life: "When your life is on course with its purpose, you are your most powerful. And you may stumble, but you will not fall."

Her words assured me that I was on course with my own purpose. Simply following my heart was where and what I was meant to be doing. It was the one thing that excited me the most even if it didn't make sense in a rational way. I was, after all, living with no fixed address, following my heart across the country in a Daisymobile, smiling at every daisy I saw on my way and travelling with a long list of big dreams.

It simply felt right. I knew that I needed to continue to follow what just felt right in life whether it meant leaving a town in search of a better campsite or buying *O Magazine*.

I finally found a picture of Ellen that day, by the way. As I began to flip through the pages of *O*, there was a full-page photo of Ellen smiling back at me. *Yes, I am indeed in the right place.*

chapter 28

The People That You Meet
When You're Walking Down the Street

Do you remember the *Sesame Street* song about the people in your neighbourhood?

One day I decided that I needed to conduct some informal sociological research and have a closer look at the cast of characters I happened to meet while walking down the street in a 24-hour period. Let me introduce you to a few of these everyday folks who appeared in my moving neighbourhood.

Estelle the Horse

I don't honestly know if her name was Estelle or not, that's just what I called her. She lived adjacent to the famous Williams Lake Stampede Grounds where I was camped one night.

I'd always been somewhat fearful of horses. As someone who had kept guppies as pets as a child, I found a 2,000-pound animal to be rather daunting. When I chatted with the campsite manager, he mentioned that Estelle was very friendly and loved being fed. I looked over at Estelle who seemed to be gazing at me affectionately. Estelle and I already had a couple of things in common. I am friendly and love being fed too.

I grabbed some grass and offered it to Estelle. She devoured it, nagging me for more. *Would you like some salsa with that Estelle? I have a tiny jar of it in my RV.* The only thing that was frightening about Estelle was the amount of grass she was able to eat. It struck me that I'd never really bothered to try understand horses until I met Estelle who captured my heart while I captured her stomach. Estelle was a special horse indeed. After only one Friday night of horsing around with her, I realized that I had nothing to be afraid of after all.

Al and Oprah

It is not often that you will meet a man with whom you can share your love of Oprah. I'd been introduced to Al by my friend Peggy, who'd suggested I venture far from my intended travelling route to meet him. I hoped he turned out to be as fun as she promised, otherwise she'd be getting the bill for the extra 587-kilometre round trip I'd be making to meet him.

Thankfully, Al lived up to Peggy's predictions. He was as fun as a man with a receding hairline in small-town British Columbia can be. We became quick friends, talking about books, work, travel and movies. The litmus test moment of our friendship appeared, however, when he showed genuine interest in watching Oprah's 20th Anniversary Collection DVD with me. *Such a man exists on the face of the earth?* Well folks, I'm pleased to say that they do.

Al and I had watched an hour or so before I turned into a pumpkin and headed back to *Miss Daisy* for a good night's sleep. I left Al on his own with Oprah, figuring he'd do what most men would do in that case, crack open a beer and turn to the sports channel or pop in an action movie. Al, however, turned out to be unlike most men.

He appeared quite tired the next morning, having stayed awake into the wee hours watching more Oprah. Imagine, I'd ventured several hundred kilometres to meet this rare breed of man—the sensitive, new age, non-sports loving, Schwarzenegger-free, Oprah-philiac guy. Instead of a bill, I sent Peggy a thank you note.

Mandy, the Haunted Doll

A visit to Quesnel is not complete until you've met Mandy.

At Al's suggestion, we headed to the Quesnel Museum and Archives late that Saturday afternoon, arriving at 4:24 p.m.

"We'll be closing in six minutes," said the clerk after greeting us. "We've switched to winter hours." *Ummm, winter doesn't begin for another three months and you could fry an egg on the sidewalk today.* The seasons and the museums work on quite a different schedule in a small town it seems.

Recognizing Al, she allowed us to wander the museum for a few minutes as she closed shop. It was then that I was able to meet Mandy, the Haunted Doll.

I'd first read about Mandy in a local travel brochure. I was quickly struck by the fact that she bore a strong resemblance to the Bride of Chuckie and wondered why she was so revered by the town.

Evidently, she has supernatural powers, one of which includes the ability to get on television. Mandy had been on the *Arsenio Hall* show a few years back. As I looked at her rather frightening appearance, I felt encouraged. If the creepy and haunted Bride of Chuckie look-a-like could enjoy her moment of fame on national television, my dream to be on the *Ellen Show* was looking promising.

Ironically, the feeling of inspiration that Mandy left me with still haunts me to this day. I mean that in a most positive way, of course.

Skully, the Tattooin' Artist

Al and I came across the 'Skull-A-Beg-Go' in a nearby parking lot. Of course, we had to take a closer look at the RV, which was adorned with an array of skulls on all sides. The bumper sticker that read "Horn Broken – Watch for Finger" added to the picture we were already painting in our minds about the owner of such a vehicle.

The Skull-A-Beg-Go was owned, not surprisingly, by a fellow named Skully who was a travelling tattooing artist from Alberta. A sign on the rig invited people inside for a tattoo. We introduced ourselves to Skully and he invited us in for a tour.

The innards of the Skull-A-Beg-Go featured an innumerable display of skull collectibles, a vintage barber chair for his tattooing artistry and a collection of items that suggested Skully had more than a few things in common with Cheech and Chong. *Miss Daisy* looked conservative by comparison and my lifestyle might have suggested, by comparison, that I had more than a few things in common with

Doris Day.

While we were a bit night and day or say, skulls and daisies in our take on life, Skully and I did share one significant thing in common. We simply wanted to live life on our terms. I'd give that approach to life a skeletal thumbs up any day.

The Gas Station Attendant

"So where's your heart taking you today?" asked the attendant at the gas station. I was about to begin driving through the Coastal Mountains of British Columbia and had pulled off for gas. I guess he'd noticed the saying on the side of *Miss Daisy*.

"I don't know yet," I replied. "I usually find out when I get there."

I'd never had anyone ask me that question before and it put a smile on my face. It's a wonderful question, one that I now ask myself each and every day.

These were just a few of the folks I'd met in the course of 24 hours. When we allow ourselves the time to get to know the people that we meet when we're walking down the street it can impact our lives in unforeseen ways. We don't have to go far to meet or to be touched by incredible people in memorable ways. They're all around us, in our own neighbourhood, each and every day.

chapter 29

The Road Back
to Daisy Creek

It had been six years since I'd last driven the stretch of highway
between Whistler and Vancouver, where the sign to Daisy Creek
sits discreetly by the side of the road. It was there that I'd adopted
my moniker 'Daisy' in what seemed to be an innocuous decision at
the time. As I look back upon it now, thank goodness I hadn't taken
my nickname after Kwakanee Creek as I really don't know how life
may have unfolded with that name. I doubt it would have been quite
the same to have driven an RV named *Miss Kwakanee* across Canada.
Daisies are far groovier than whatever a Kwakanee is and it seemed
to be that the whole daisy thing was just synchronously meant to be.

Curiously, it wasn't too long after I first set eyes on Daisy Creek
before more daisies began to spread like wildflowers throughout my
life.

You've likely had it happen. Friends and family catch wind of
something you're interested in and before you know it, on every
major holiday or special occasion you're being gifted with an item
related to your interest. This is how, in the months that followed my
trip to Whistler, I became the owner of an entire house filled with
daisy paraphernalia that included tea towels, dishware, paintings, hats

and t-shirts, a daisy finger puppet and more.

I planted wild daisies in my front garden and when the time came to choose a name for my bed and breakfast, I chose 'A Wild Daisy'. It was as if my life had been hit by a flash mob of daisies, but I didn't mind at all as I felt comforted in the company of my vibrant white and yellow petalled friends. And only a few years later I would be enjoying my biggest and most fun daisy friend of all, *Miss Daisy*.

~

It was a bit of an emotional trip down daisy memory lane as I drove *Miss Daisy* along the Sea to Sky highway, passing the sign for Daisy Creek. I turned off the road and parked. I had not stopped here years ago, not knowing then what I know now, and I wanted to give my thanks for its role in my life.

 It was a gorgeous September day and the water on the lake glistened and danced in the sunshine. I stood on a cliff overlooking Daisy Lake, pausing to savour and ponder all that cascaded from the decision of a moment to take a nickname from a tiny sign at the side of the road. I couldn't help but smile as I joked to the spirit of the lake, "Hey, check out my daisy thing now! It keeps getting bigger!"

At the same time, I wondered why life had led me here six years before. And why it had brought me back here again, after a meandering and unusual path in life. It had all begun so simply, by taking on the nickname, 'Daisy.' It did seem rather remarkable that a few daisy-filled years later I'd be enjoying a cross-Canada trip in a giant Daisymobile.

"What is it all about?" I wondered to myself.

A second later, two hawks circled overhead as if they'd heard my call. Did these visitors from the animal realm hold the answer to my question? Some quick research on animal totems in Native American cultures assured me that their appearance was a good sign.

In native cultures the hawk represents a messenger who often appears in our life when we need to pay attention to the subtle messages found in our surroundings and from those we come in contact with. *Pay attention Heather.*

The hawk is also a bird of the heavens, orchestrating the changes necessary for our spiritual growth. *Don't worry Heather, we'll guide you on your journey.*

Hawks see the overall view and people having this totem are aware of omens and spirit messages. *Heather, just keep following the daisies.*

When you have this totem, you will be aware of and work towards fulfilling your soul's purpose. *Heather, you're doing the most important work you'll ever do in life, your soul's work.*

I understood the hawk's messages. *Heather, about the whole daisy thing? It's all part of your bigger life picture, so keep with it and keep your eyes peeled for daisies.* I knew somewhere in my heart that my journey to Daisy Creek and Daisy Lake, my daisy-filled life and my trip with *Miss Daisy* were no small coincidence. The hawks simply wanted me to understand the bigger daisy picture, as crazy as it may have appeared at times.

All I needed to do was to keep following daisies and to be sure to stop and enjoy each one as it came along.

chapter 30

You Are Never Too Old to Dream a New Dream

Heather, what the heck are you doing?

I'd just left mainland Canada behind. But I hadn't anticipated that doubt might be my first thought upon landing in Nanaimo on Vancouver Island. Not that I'd expected a parade and fireworks, either of which would have been lovely, I simply hadn't expected that I'd feel as nervous as a five-year-old heading off to Mrs. Petryshyn's primary grade class for the first time.

Maybe it was the recollection of the conversation I'd had recently with the clerk at the counter while trying to renew my health insurance card. He had asked me where I lived, a question that can leave a Daisymobile driver who's following her heart in a bit of a conundrum.

"Well, that's a good question," I replied. "I'm from Ottawa, my mailing address is at my mom's house and I'm roving across the country in a daisy-covered RV. I'm following my heart wherever it takes me." That was not the answer he was looking for, judging by the perturbed expression on his face. Bureaucratic types seem to have an annoying fixation with fixed addresses.

Maybe it was the fact that it was cold and raining in Nanaimo and I'd awoken to the chilly realization that my warm and comfy fall wardrobe was back in my storage unit in Ottawa. Maybe it was the realization that I'd made my way to an island where I'd be spending the winter and that there was no turning back now. Or maybe it was (d) All of the Above.

As much as I am a proponent of following my heart, taking risks and making big changes in life, on that particular day I'd wondered what the heck I'd done with my comfortable world.

~

The two sides of my personality launched into a vigorous debate about my situation. One side argued that it was perfectly normal to feel a bit of fear and trepidation. Leaving the mainland had marked another leap of faith into the unknown and more changes were undoubtedly on the horizon. This side also reasoned that I was precisely where I needed to be, that discomfort longs to become comfort and, if all else fails, there's always comfort to be found in a good piece of cake. Between tears, the other side of me was entertaining the thought of driving back to Ottawa, having an emotional reunion with my fall wardrobe and settling under a permanent roof—and eating cake.

My willpower and commitment to fulfilling my goals and dreams was being tested. It was similar to the experience I'd had a few years back, when nearing the finish line of a 42 km marathon event.

I had trained for four months leading up to event day. I was firmly committed to the challenge of completing my first-ever marathon, although I will candidly admit that my favourite part of training was the waffle breakfast after my Sunday workout with friends.

After 16 Sundays of waffles, event day had finally arrived. A marathon carries its own mix of emotions. Anticipation, excitement and memories of waffles carried me across the start line and through the first half of the event. It was in the latter half that I began to question why I'd signed up for a marathon in the first place.

At the 37 km mark, my body was aching and my feet were sore. Conversation between my running companions and I began to take on a geriatric-sounding tone. "My back hurts. My hip is sore. My knee is killing me. My haemorrhoids are flaring up again." Yet, I was as committed to pushing through the discomfort and crossing the finish line as I was to trying to save that kind of conversation until I'd hit my eighties.

From somewhere, somehow, came the willpower to push through those uncomfortable final kilometres. My haemorrhoids and I crossed the finish line of our first marathon together only two minutes above my goal time. These are the kinds of miracles that can happen simply by adding more waffles to your life.

In Nanaimo, I felt as if I'd arrived at the 37 km mark of my RV marathon adventure too. My haemorrhoids weren't causing any problems, but I also hadn't been following my weekly waffle regimen. I was feeling a bit uncomfortable, maybe because I couldn't see the finish line of my dreams and I wasn't quite sure what challenges lay ahead.

I decided that I needed a walk to sort out my thoughts.

~

The sun had broken through the clouds, which provided a sense of levity to my situation. Without knowing the neighbourhood, I simply began to walk, venturing along the nearby streets until I found myself glancing at a glorious view of the ocean. *Heather, what the heck are you doing here?* I walked on, hoping that an answer would come from somewhere.

Two deer that were grazing in someone's front yard stared back at me. *Do you know why I'm here?* Either their mouths were full or they were too engrossed in their own raison d'être to respond. An older woman, Audrey, saw me watching the deer and stopped to say hello. Audrey told me that most locals considered the deer to be pests as they tended to eat their way through the neighbourhood. *Gee, imagine what the deer would think if they ever saw humans at a buffet table?*

Audrey and I chatted for a few minutes about life in Nanaimo. Then she pointed me in the direction of three beach access points so I could visit the ocean side.

We parted ways and I continued my walk, coming to one of the access points she'd mentioned. Curious, I walked to the entrance and saw a lengthy stairway leading to the water. My legs quivered at the idea of taking the stairs. What goes down must come back up and my leg muscles were still angry at me for the two-hour uphill hike I'd taken them on the day before. A bench with a lovely view of the ocean caught my eye as a perfect spot to spend a few minutes in thought and rest. I'd learned by now to not only follow my heart, but also to follow my legs wherever they took me or, in this case, wherever they didn't want to take me.

I walked towards the bench and noticed that it was adorned with a commemorative plaque. A smile crossed my lips as I read it. Then I sat down on the bench, realizing that my answer had come. The plaque read, "You are never too old to dream a new dream."

Thank goodness for the message that there's no age restriction on the fulfilment of dreams! I had to laugh and smile at the timing of the message as it had arrived on the eve of my 46th birthday. Imagine if the dream cut-off age had been 45? Would I have received a letter in the mail?

"Dear Heather, we regret to inform you that as you have surpassed the age of 45, you are far too old to dream and thus we are no longer able to fulfil your dream requests. We apologize for an inconvenience this may cause but we are happy to enclose one of our complimentary pens. Dreamily Yours, The Gang at the Magical Dream Place Headquarters."

Thankfully the gang at the Magical Dream Place Headquarters don't care how many candles are on my birthday cake. They just want me to have my cake and dream it too.

I was not too old to dream a new dream. I was not too old to create a new life. I was not too old to be who I was truly meant to be. That's why I had landed on the island! This knowledge was a wonderful gift and useful reminder to receive on my birthday. As I headed back to *Miss Daisy* that afternoon, I swear I heard the sounds of a mystical choir singing in the distance, "Happy Birthday to Heather, Happy Birthday to Heather...." I suspect that it was the gang over at the Magical Dream Place Headquarters up to their usual shenanigans, once again.

chapter 31

A Change of Heart

"You had me at Nanaimo bar," I said to my new friend Penny, somewhat jokingly, as she showed me around Nanaimo one day.

I am hopelessly addicted to the sinfully delicious three-layered dessert bar that is the ultimate marriage of chocolate, coconut, nuts, butter, sugar, custard and fun. Nanaimo bars have the transformational dessert power to transport you from here to Cloud Nine in a nanosecond. My sweet tooth was notably excited when I informed it we were headed to Nanaimo, where folklore has it that the legendary bar has its origins and where many others have also fallen in love at first bite.

Penny had greeted me with a Nanaimo bar the day she picked me up for a tour of the town. She was a clever tour guide and town ambassador, kicking things off on such a tempting and tasty note.

Upon my arrival in Nanaimo, many questions and logistics remained to sort out in terms of living on the island for the winter. I'd already tentatively reserved myself a spot in an RV park in Victoria, the most southern city on the Island and known to be the warmest place in Canada in the winter.

I'd forgotten about the fact that Victoria is also often referred to as the town of "the newly wed and nearly dead." Upon learning that the minimum age of entry for the recreational hall at the RV park was 55, I began to suspect that I might not share the same demographic profile as my potential RVing neighbours shall I say. It's one thing to discuss haemorrhoids and bodily aches and pains during a marathon, I was not yet at the stage of life where I wished to discuss such topics over a game of bingo or during dinner.

Once I'd thoroughly licked any remnants of Nanaimo bar off my fingers, Penny and I kicked off our tour of Nanaimo by making a visit to an ocean-side park and the downtown seawall, which offers a beautiful view of the harbour. No tour of Nanaimo would have been complete without a stop in at one of the 472 pubs in town, so we graciously obliged.

With visions of Nanaimo bars dancing through my head and 471 pubs still left to visit, Nanaimo was beginning to look promising whereas Victoria was quickly beginning to lose ground.

The question still remained as to where *Miss Daisy* and I could park ourselves and whether we'd be comfortable in Nanaimo's winter climate. Life aligned beautifully to answer those questions as Penny knew the owners of one of the local RV campsites. We headed there on a reconnaissance mission of sorts.

Things were looking positive as we drove into the park. The campsite grounds were nicely forested and a mere two-minute walk to a nearby lake and hiking trails. A quick glance around revealed neither a set of bingo cards nor a Shoprider in sight. The icing on the proverbial daisy cake came in the form of a handmade candleholder in the office that was decorated with large wild daisies. My already partially changed mind would need no further coaxing, my heart had sent me a clear message. *Heather, Nanaimo is the right place for you.*

A Nanaimo bar here, an ocean there, a pub here, a daisy there … I think that's sometimes how the best decisions are made. Circumstances easily fall into place and it just feels right. Maybe the reason I was initially drawn to Victoria was a sense of familiarity. It was a city that shared many similarities to my former Ottawa. Nanaimo was unknown territory where I'd be living an existence I'd not known before, in my RV, near a lake in the woods, in winter. Yet on my quest for new dreams and new possibilities, my heart surely knew that I wouldn't find them in a place where I'd looked before. They'd only be found by going to places I had not yet been.

But, truthfully, between you and I, Penny really did have me at Nanaimo bar.

chapter 32

Beginning Another Beginning

I have a thing with new socks. I don't know how, when or why it originated but at some point in the course of my lifetime I began to hoard packages of new socks. I love adding to my precious vault of inventory, which has moved with me several times over the years. Many brand-new pairs had accompanied me across Canada, remaining safely untouched the entire journey. While I discovered that I was not too old to dream a new dream, perhaps I was too old to open a pair of new socks. Either that or I needed a session with a pop sockologist to cure me of my illness.

Nonetheless, new socks and new dreams cannot be compared. I did not want my new dreams to remain un-opened as many of my socks had for years and years. I had begun to dream big new dreams as I travelled across the country with *Miss Daisy*. It is one thing however to dream a new dream, it is another to create and wear that dream.

"Heather, it's time to believe," advised several insightful friends on a brief return visit to Ottawa later that October. I had a suitcase full of big dreams, which I now needed to fill with unwavering belief that they would come true. I realized that I'd been missing that part of the equation.

There would now be a new part to my journey, one that would bring new changes, new discomforts and a few new risks. The unknowns would continue to change as would the nature of my journey as I transitioned from my mobile lifestyle to a stationary RV park existence.

This second leg of the journey would take me across Canada in a slightly less glamorous vehicle, my, 10-year-old SUV which I'd left back in Ottawa earlier in the summer. It's ironic how life will sometimes send us down the same road again if we need to. Perhaps I needed a new perspective. I had had plenty of time to reflect upon the wisdom of my heart during my travels with *Miss Daisy*. This second trip would allow me opportunity to reflect upon the need to believe. I would have to be sure to pack belief in my suitcase this time around, right next to all of my socks.

~

'Twas the night before hitting the road and it felt like Nadia Comaneci was performing an Olympic gymnastics routine inside my stomach. I felt nervous, scared, excited and slightly overwhelmed. A melting pot of emotions swirled within me as I pondered the road ahead.

Things felt different this time around. When I departed Ottawa in July with *Miss Daisy*, I'd planned to return to Ottawa permanently in October. I am showing my naiveté when I admit that I had some kind of ending in mind to an adventure of the heart. No such thing exists! I know better now. I had made it back to Ottawa indeed, but only to pack up my vehicle and my winter clothes to head back to Nanaimo.

This was a new beginning of a different sort. There was no end-point in sight and no timeline in mind. I was not sure if or when I might return to Ottawa again. Goodbye to the comfort of a city and friends I knew well for a town and a future that I didn't know well at all.

However, the tug of my heartstrings and the lure of an endless supply of Nanaimo bars was stronger than the discomfort of a few intestinal somersaults. Nanaimo called me for whatever adventure it had in store.

"Heather, there's great stuff awaiting you in Nanaimo. Yes, you don't know what it is yet. Just trust this it is there for you. It's just waiting for you to arrive. You're heading off to a big surprise party organized by the guru of event planners, your very own heart." This dose of sage advice from a good friend helped calm my nerves.

I liked that perspective and I gladly embraced it. Venturing off to a big surprise party is much more appealing that simply venturing into the unknown. My stomach seemed to be far more excited about that idea as well. *We're going to a surprise party? CAKE! That means CAKE!* With that piece of news, my stomach had gleefully begun to dream a dream of its own.

Like dreams, you're never too old to enjoy more cake.

chapter 33

I've Looked at Life
from Both Sides Now...

Only a few hours into my cross-Canada drive, version 2.0, and I was already missing having an on-board refrigerator and my own toilet—and my giant jar of salsa. My SUV lacked some of the luxuries that *Miss Daisy* had offered, including the ability to indulge in heavenly naps at the side of the road on a real bed. The SUV offered a few advantages of its own however; I never had to worry about getting stuck under a bridge and it was approximately 15,000 per cent cheaper to fill at the pumps than dear *Miss Daisy*.

I was beginning to look at life from both sides now, which shouldn't have been all that surprising since that was what Joni Mitchell was crooning about on the CD player as I drove. I had chosen some different travelling companions for this trip and it was Joni who serenaded me as I headed into Northern Ontario that foggy morning along Lake Superior.

As the fog began to lift, my thoughts took me back to the year before. It was at that time that my intuitive friend Tara told me, amongst other things, that I would be selling my house in Ottawa and moving out west. I had laughed at her prediction and didn't believe her. I had absolutely no intention or plan to sell my house at the time. Nor did I have any plans to move out west. I simply didn't believe in the possibility and completely dismissed the idea.

Now guess who had the last laugh on that one?

I was beginning to look at belief from both sides now (sorry Joni). Things I had once thought as impossible had not only become possible, they'd become realities.

As I drove, I took an inventory of some of my former beliefs that had changed in recent months:

- I used to believe that RVs were a lazy way to camp and had said that I'd never buy one. Interesting that I'd made these remarks before ever having tried RVing! Now I think that RVing is a fantastic way to travel.

- I used to believe that I had to seek love from outside of myself, that some magical person would come into my life and rescue me from me. Now I believe that love starts with me and from within.

- I used to believe that life was hard work and a struggle. I now believe that life is meant to be fun and flow relatively easily. Even challenges have a greater divine purpose and are part of the same journey.

- I never used to believe in a Higher Power, God, Creator, whatever you want to call it. Now I can't imagine not believing in something greater than myself that guides my life.

- I used to believe I couldn't be as smart or successful as other people. Once I began to ask, *Well, why not?* I began to appreciate my own abilities.

- I never used to notice wild daisies. Now I believe they're the most inspirational, powerful and groovy flower around. As well as being my best friend and guide.

Sadly, there was only one thing that had ever stood between believing and not believing.

The common denominator was me.

Joni's words echoed in the back of my mind, "...things I would have done but clouds got in the way...." I used to allow the clouds of my own fears, beliefs, or limited perspective get in my own way. To lift myself above the clouds, I couldn't let any doubt get in the way of my dreams any longer.

When I looked at some past beliefs and examined my own contradictions, it was time to ask myself some powerful questions. *How can I not believe in things I cannot see? How can I not believe in bigger possibilities? How can I not believe in the power of my own dreams? Heather, just look at how some of your old beliefs have already been transformed. Don't set limits on yourself.* Life had already begun to lead me down the pathway of belief. I trusted that it would continue to guide me and hold my hand as I leapt towards bigger dreams.

In true daisy fashion, believing did not disappoint me.

~

As I approached Thunder Bay, I decided to stop there for the night rather than continue to my originally planned destination, Kenora, a few hours away. It was a beautiful, sunny day and I decided to enjoy a bike ride in a city that captivates my heart. After checking into my hotel, I headed out on a route that I'd travelled in the summer that paralleled the shores of Lake Superior and ended at a beautiful lakeside park.

Now, there was a dusting of snow along my route that day and, judging by the roadside foliage, most areas had clearly been hit by frost. Thus, I was remarkably surprised by what greeted me at the park entrance. There stood a single wild daisy in full bloom, strong, lively and tall. I hadn't seen a daisy since August and yet here was one, and only one, in Northern Ontario at the end of a frosty October. I wouldn't have believed it was possible, but the proof was flourishing before my eyes.

I smiled at the daisy and it spoke back to me, loudly and clearly, "Heather, Believe."

chapter 34

A Heavenly Night at
the Christian Motel

I hadn't been to church in years yet somehow I'd found my way to a
Christian motel in Brandon, Manitoba.

While standing at the front desk waiting to register, I turned to see
a large bulletin board filled with numerous thank you, holiday and
best wishes cards from past guests. Judging from the comments, it
seemed that guests had obviously enjoyed their stay at the Midway
Motel.

"Thanks for the wonderful stay!"

"We can't wait to visit again. The cat makes me feel at home."

Several guests seemed to appreciate that this was a 'Christian' motel
as one of the cards had indicated. "Thanks for the lovely stay, it's so
nice to stay in a Christian motel," it read.

What qualifies a motel as a Christian motel? Are you guaranteed a heavenly
night's sleep? Would I see the face of Jesus on my pillow or on a grilled cheese
sandwich?

While I would not call myself a Christian, I felt very much ease in a motel that had some sort of spiritual consciousness to it. My beliefs are more like a spiritual smoothie, a blend of several things that I think are good for me.

However, I didn't mind the framed biblical passages on the walls of each room, which formed part of the Christian character. They were a nice contrast to the signs I'd seen in my motel room back in Northern Ontario that read, "Please don't clean your fish in your room." *Well gosh, where's a girl to clean her fish if not in her motel room?* Apparently Christians don't need to be reminded of this simple rule of motel etiquette.

I don't know if it's a strange coincidence or what but I did enjoy a most divine sleep the night of my stay at the Christian motel.

~

No day of mine starts without breakfast and coffee. So the next morning I headed to the dining room where I met fellow guests Alice, Ted and Rick. The two requisite traveller's questions followed: "Where are you from?" and "Where are you going?"

"I'm headed to Vancouver Island," I said.

Alice and Ted looked at each other and exchanged some sort of knowing smile.

"Once people from Ontario get on the Island, they don't go back," they predicted.

Whether that would be true in my case, I didn't yet know but, nonetheless, over breakfast the four of us discussed the merits of various Canadian geographic locations.

Ted and Alice were a retired couple who'd been married for 51 years. They'd spent their entire lifetime in Saskatchewan, growing up in Regina where they owned a large acreage of farmland.

"We love to travel, but we wouldn't live anywhere else but Saskatchewan."

"I love the prairies, the openness of the sky and the endless horizons," I shared with them.

Alice smiled. She admitted that for quite some time she'd taken the beauty of the prairies for granted. It was only when a visiting friend commented on the splendour and vastness of the prairies that her perspective shifted. Alice had not fully stopped to appreciate the beauty that surrounded her. Her friend's remarks provided the gentle tap on the shoulder she needed to feel grateful for what she had in her prairie home.

How many of us are just like Alice, having lived somewhere for years, unaware or unappreciative of the beauty all around us?

Rick was a native of Brandon who declared that he had no intentions of ever moving back to Manitoba. He'd found a new home that he loved in Alberta, where he worked up in oil and gas country. Like many young Canadians, he'd been lured to Fort McMurray, in northern Alberta, where the promise of making good money was irresistible. While thumbing through the Brandon newspaper as we chatted, Rick laughed, "Now there's something you won't see up in Fort McMurray … obituaries!" That was likely true enough as the average age in Fort McMurray is likely in the mid-30s.

My conversation with fellow travellers at the Christian motel had left its impression on me. There is no one place to call home. There is no one way to live. There is no one-size-fits-all formula when it comes to choosing a place to live. Geographically, spiritually, emotionally, you simply have to find that place in life that feels right for you—a place that makes your heart sing.

"I'm on my way," I said as I bid farewell to my friends at the Christian motel and hit the road again that morning. *I'm on my way to wherever that place may be.*

chapter 35

The Aliens Land on Planet Nanaimo

Two days later I arrived in Nanaimo where I was happily re-united with *Miss Daisy*.

Finding someone to RV-sit your rig while you're out of town can pose a bit of a challenge. Fortunately, I found the ideal candidate in the father of a friend who was an avid hunter. He'd taken down not just one but two moose in the most recent hunting season. If anyone had the qualifications to take care of *Miss Daisy* while I was away, it was Ted. Securely parked on his property, I had no doubt that he'd be happy to use anyone who might dare go near *Miss Daisy* as target practice.

My friend Tina met me at the ferry, helping to co-ordinate my next move. We enjoyed a beer and some homemade moose sausage with Ted before driving *Miss Daisy* to the RV park. Filled with excitement and anticipation, I pulled into campsite #42 and stepped out to give my big fibreglass friend a hug and a kiss. I wanted to reassure her that she'd be fine, well, that *we'd* be fine in our new town. We both felt somewhat nervous with the change to our lives.

Thank goodness that my friend Tina was there with me, once again.

~

Tina and I had met a couple of years back in Ottawa, while working together at an outdoor gear store. We shared much in common; we attended the same university, loved the outdoors and enjoyed a healthy appetite for post-work beer and nachos. Our bond went much deeper than that however. When we met back in 2008, both of us were asking some bigger questions of life, but we didn't know any of the answers. We bonded as seekers and soul sisters on some sort of spiritual quest to who-knows-where.

In the midst of our ponderings, an Anglican minister friend of Tina's suggested that we join a five-week discussion group she was hosting on the poetry of the Sufi mystic, Rumi. When Tina suggested the class to me I hadn't even heard of Rumi nor had I set foot in a church for years. I thought that a whirling dervish, which I will say quite simplistically is a dancing Sufi, sounded like a fun name for some sort of chocolate-covered, dollop-shaped marshmallow treat. *How the heck is studying Sufi poetry going to help me figure out my life?* It seemed like trying to quench my thirst by taking a nap. I did not see the correlation.

Nonetheless, shortly thereafter, some inexplicable force landed both Tina and I inside a downtown church discussing the poetry of Rumi and Sufi mysticism. Each week, we'd head out for a beer after class and, more often than not, discuss the mysticism as to how two non-church-going non-poets had ended up in such a predicament.

No one was more surprised than we were when we suddenly began to write poetry. I'd barely passed my English literature class in high school. The only poems I'd created to date had been some cheesy rhymes I'd written inside homemade greeting cards.

Yet poems flowed out of me and I had no idea where they came from. I wouldn't have recognized them as my own except for the fact that it was indeed me who was wielding the pen as I frantically wrote. They seemed to come from a place within myself that I had never known before.

One particular poem remains my favourite. It was the first poem that I wrote after our first week of class. Perhaps the reference to the hillside either spoke to my heart or foreshadowed my eventual destination near the mountains of the west coast.

Upon the Hillside

Be still.
Listen to your breathing.
Life force emanates from your heart.
Let the sun rise through your being.

This is a place of peace and joy
Fear does not reside here.
Love is in continual transit.

Truth and essence visit you often
Companions of destiny come calling
Life flows freely, your home knows no doors.

Extend your hospitality
And share in the bountiful feast upon your table.
There are no limits to your offerings.

This is your residence
Upon the hillside.

Both Tina and I thoroughly enjoyed our time with Rumi. Even being back in a church basement brought evoked childhood memories of Saturday night community church bingo parties, egg salad sandwiches, Mrs. Audley's homemade chocolate brownies and all-you-can-drink Kool-Aid.

My time with Rumi didn't lead to the answers to my questions, not directly anyways. It seemed instead to lead to further questions. *How do I create the life that I truly want? How can I be happy? Who am I, why am I here and what am I about? How can I make my dreams come true?*

Again, life didn't respond with a direct answer. Instead, it sent me off on a life-changing RV adventure that eventually landed me on Planet Nanaimo.

On the other hand, perhaps that was the answer to all of my questions.

~

Tina had arrived in Nanaimo earlier that summer after opportunity had come knocking on her door. She'd been offered a six-month house-sitting gig at a time in her life when she was also in need of more change. Much like myself, Tina also experienced moments of wondering what the heck she'd done to her life by agreeing to head to Nanaimo.

"Heather, it's like I've landed in the Twilight Zone," she'd forewarned me before my initial visit of 'her' house. My jaw still dropped as we drove up to the front gates and I caught my initial glimpse. Nestled in the hills, the property was laden with trees, several Martha Stewart-esque gardens, decorative antiques, a large pond with a boardwalk and a relaxing view of the adjacent winery. Besides the main house, there were horse stables, a recreation facility housing a pool table, fitness equipment and bar, and Tina's lodging, which was a cute log cabin tucked in the woods that offered an idyllic view of the pond and its resident waterfowl.

Tina and I stood in the middle of her Twilight Zone that day, discussing the bizarre chain of events that had aligned to land us together in Nanaimo. The realities of our lives were so different from where we'd come from it was as though we'd been abducted by spiritual aliens and transported to another planet.

We still had many questions about life, although the questions had begun to change since our church-basement Rumi days. And we both hoped that as we ventured further afield on the somewhat surreal Planet Nanaimo, that some answers would begin to appear.

Naive of me I know, to think that life would have taken us on a more direct route than the ones we'd travelled before.

chapter 36

Why Wiggling is Good for You

The chances are exceedingly high that you will never, ever, ever, ever see me on the hit TV show *So You Think You Can Dance*. I am under no delusions of grandeur about my dancing skills or lack thereof. Nor will I ever be mistaken for the woman in Flashdance. I'm as agile as a lumbering elephant, but I don't let that stop me. I simply love to dance.

Dancing excites and energizes me in a way that other things don't. Well, except for all things chocolate and coffee. When I'm dancing I feel my soul come alive and I feel connected to something beyond myself. Some folks meditate to connect with their spirit, but mine seems to prefer to bust out some (albeit uncoordinated) dance moves.

I discovered an even deeper connection to both music and dancing while venturing with *Miss Daisy*. Maybe I'd found my perfect dance partner in my travelling companion. Snuggled into our campsite each night, I'd turn the music up loud and shake my groove thing around the tiny living space. Of course, I did draw the curtains for privacy. I drew enough attention with *Miss Daisy's* decal job; I didn't need to attract a crowd of people coming to see the dancing elephant show inside the Daisymobile.

When I danced, I felt great. I could feel a new energy awaken within. My body and mind flowed into some other place where my thoughts and dreams could wander, play and begin to grow.

I wasn't simply following my heart anymore. I was dancing my heart out too.

~

"Dancing reveals your true power," the voice whispered to me. I'd been having many dreams lately in which an ethereal voice spoke to me before quickly vanishing. It was like being tuned into my own spiritual radio. I awoke in my hotel room feeling energized, filled with purpose and ready to get my wiggle on.

The timing couldn't have been better since I had travelled to Vancouver for a fitness conference and was registered for a workshop on Groovin', a new form of exercise that infuses dance, intuitive movement and so much more.

When I met Misty, our workshop facilitator, it was obvious that I wouldn't need a coffee that morning. She had more than enough innate battery power to keep me and the entire group going all on her own. Dressed in an ear-to-ear smile, her trademark dreadlocks and buzzing with effervescence, she was an immediately likeable spirit.

"I just want to get people to wiggle!" she said of her life mission. I was in the right place. I wasn't a dancer but I could certainly wiggle, which is a far more appropriate term for the type of movements I put to music. I like it when fancy sounding things get dressed down, they become so much more accessible and fun-sounding too.

"Wiggling is about freeing your mind and spirit. It's about dancing YOUR dance, each and every day of your life. When you wiggle, you'll find your true self and your true power." she said. I had bit of a Twilight Zone moment. *Had she whispered those words in my ear that morning?*

I'd always known that wiggling was fun and felt great. I began to understand however, that wiggling had even more power and wisdom to it. Wiggling would help me find the true Me and maybe it would help me create a groovy life too.

I told Misty about my RV adventure and mentioned that I liked to wiggle with *Miss Daisy*. She then shared an impressive statistic with me. Everything she'd ever thought or dreamed about while dancing had always come true. Wowza! That's a statistic that is worth wiggling about!

Maybe those Sufis and whirling dervishes were onto something after all. They danced for hours and hours to connect to God and to their own higher spiritual calling. Maybe they'd even nudged me along in my own dancing pursuits. Ironically, I had only begun to introduce random acts of wiggling into my life after spending time with some Sufis in a church basement not long ago.

~

The music played loudly as we wiggled and jiggled our way around the room.

"Just feel the music, be a free spirit, get crazy, you're just dancing for the health of it!" Misty shouted. I moved and I grooved. I wiggled and I jiggled. And I let myself be Me on the dance floor. No hiding behind a curtain or worrying about what others might think.
I could feel my true power began to reveal itself on the dance floor.

That's why wiggling is good for you.

It helps you begin your own dance in life.

It helps you learn to be comfortable in your own dancing shoes.

It teaches you to dance through daily life in your own way.

It helps you dance to the beat of your own heart.

I don't think life is meant to be overly complicated. It makes sense that when you wiggle a bit, life will wiggle with you. And from there, it's as simple as following your wiggle wherever it takes you.

chapter 37

Lost and Not Yet Found

There are bad hair days. And then there are the "What the heck happened on the top of your head?" hair days. Unfortunately, I was having one of the latter.

I'd arrived in Nanaimo in need of a haircut. As a female with short hair, I am somewhat particular about how my hair is cut. It needs to be feminine, cut in layers and kept stylish. I asked a new friend if she knew anyone who was, I specified with great specificity, "good with short hair."

"Oh yes," she said. "Go see my guy James, he's been doing my hair for years and he's fantastic."

"Great," I said, foolishly overlooking the fact that she had long, straight hair.

I arrived for my appointment to be greeted by James, whom I quickly discovered was nearly completely bald. I wouldn't trust a dentist with no teeth but there I was, about to leave my precious hair in the hands of a man who had none. The writing was on the bald wall that this might not be the greatest haircut of my life. Sadly, that was a gross understatement for what turned out to be a rather hair-raising experience.

James began cutting away and chatting while assuring me that he was a perfectionist of his art. I am not sure that I'd call his technique artful. He had all the finesse of the Grim Reaper taking a scythe to my mane.

I have two major cowlicks on my head and if there's anything I've learned from my cowlicks over the years, it's to go with the flow. Trying to fight the power of a cowlick is like trying to get Homer Simpson to stop eating donuts. Some things just won't change.

One of my cowlicks resides at the front of my head and for years, I've parted my hair in such a clever manner as to conceal its presence. Nonetheless, James seemed to love a challenge so suggested that I try parting my hair on the other side of my head. For 46 years, my hair had gone in one direction but there was Captain James Kirk, suggesting that my hair could boldly go where it'd had never gone before.

"Um, okay," I said hesitantly, trying to be polite but not overly convinced of the brilliance of his idea. If his name had been Moses I'd have felt far more confident that he could pull off this sort of parting miracle.

James brought out the blow dryer and gel to wrestle my unco-operative cowlick into place. The feisty gal wouldn't go down easily. James would also somehow need to reverse the whirlpool of a lifelong cowlick on the back of my head to pull this feat off. He would have been better off recruiting an entire SWAT hair tactical unit to tame my cowlick beasts.

James huffed and puffed with the blow dryer, trying to bring my cowlicks down. The end result had me looking as if I'd lost a fight with a weedwhacker.

"It's lopsided," said my friend during my first public appearance with my grotesquely revised head of hair. Indeed, my hair was listing to one side. A giant lump of hair stuck out of the right side of my head as a swoop of bangs kept trying to counter the will of my feisty cowlick. The hair around my ears had been mercilessly and masculinely chopped, earning me the right to dub my new style, 'The Man Cut'. If only I had a walk-on role in a horror movie, it would have been the perfect cut.

The Man Cut will go down in history as the worst haircut of my life. Yet somehow it seemed to fit my circumstances at the time. More than just my hair wasn't flowing smoothly those first few weeks after landing in Nanaimo.

~

My Self was definitely feeling uncomfortable during my initial weeks in Nanaimo, as I'd taken yet another leap into the unfamiliar. Life was very different than it had been over the summer. In addition to my Man Cut, it rained monsoon-style every day, *Miss Daisy* and I were no longer on the move, and I got lost on a regular basis while driving around town.

I awoke one morning feeling overwhelmed by my life. So I don't know why I decided that it was a good time to try tofurkey, simulated turkey sausage made with tofu, for the first time.

I'd wanted to change my diet and explore more vegetarian options so when I saw a package of tofurkey in the grocery store I brought it home. My meal of tofurkey, tomato sauce and whole wheat noodles, washed down with soy milk as unrelenting rain pounded on the roof of *Miss Daisy*, did not provide the comfort that I needed. *What the tofurkey was I thinking?*

It was another valuable life lesson. When you're going through big changes in life, call on old friends like pot roast, lasagne, chicken casserole or apple pie to help get you through. Save the tofurkey for your good hair days.

~

I was a bit of a lost soul, literally and figuratively. On most of those early excursions around town, I spent at least half of my travel time lost and feeling frustrated that I didn't know my way around. I considered putting a sign on myself: "If found, please return to the Westwood Lake RV Park."

The upside to getting lost regularly was that I had time to reflect upon change. That was certainly the case after I spent 30 minutes circling town, trying to find my way home one rainy evening. I'd just been to see *Cherry Blossoms*, a German film that tells the story of Trudi and Rudi, her husband. Rudi liked his routine in life—he went to work at the same time every day, ate the same lunch and worked for the same company all of his life. He loathed change and the unfamiliar. *Here's a tip for you Rudi, don't go see James for a haircut!* Trudi finds out that Rudi has a terminal illness and takes Rudi to visit their children in the German countryside. After Trudi dies unexpectedly, Rudi decides to honour her unfulfilled desires in life and heads to Japan to see Mt. Fuji and learn about Butoh dancing.

Heading to Japan was a huge stretch of an adventure for Rudi; he struggled with the vast changes in culture, scenery, language and loss of his wife. It was a tectonic shift in his reality and experience. As I watched scenes in which he first found himself investigating the streets of Tokyo, overwhelmed by his encounters and wearing a somewhat dazed expression on his face, I empathized with Rudi. I felt somewhat dazed too. At least in Nanaimo, I enjoyed familiar language and culture albeit a very foreign-looking hairdo.

Rudi's Japan experience pushed out his boundaries and he emerged a very different man. As I circled Nanaimo that evening trying to find my way home, I felt lifted by Rudi's story. It clarified the 'why' of my own adventure, one that had pushed out my boundaries in many ways as well.

Like Rudi, I too wanted to emerge from my discomfort a very different person.

~

I had obviously not yet learned from the tofurkey incident, otherwise I would not have also signed up for my first-ever improv acting workshop that same week. Thinking it would enhance my public-speaking and creative-thinking skills, I'd eagerly registered for the session.

In keeping with my directionally challenged week, I got lost twice on my way to the Spotlight Academy. With tears flowing down my cheeks, I finally arrived at the doorstep. I had endured enough change and discomfort for the week. I wasn't aware that more was still to come.

Alan, the workshop facilitator welcomed me. After introductions, I discovered that I was the only non-actor in the group. *Well, I'm already this far out of my element, I may as well keep going.*

Alan warmed us up with a few basic improv exercises designed to loosen our bodies and brains. In my case, I might have been better off downing a couple of shots of Scotch. He wanted us to reach that point of 'flowing in the now' as we tossed a ball around in a circle, uttering random words and sounds with each pass. I dance with the grace of an elephant and I felt equally as awkward doing improv. Nonetheless, I was intrigued by the parallels that Alan drew between improv and life.

He spoke of those brilliant moments when you see an actor

'intuiting' their role, allowing divinity to flow through them in their performance. When doing improv, you remove your intellect and simply respond in the moment. You must also practice removing old patterns and being open to receiving and giving in completely new ways. You must become absolutely fearless.

I seemed to be facing the same challenges with improv that I was facing in life.

I was literally tongue-tied during one exercise in which we were asked to speak in gibberish while volleying a story back and forth with a partner. *Hey, I'm not a politician so it's not as if I'd ever spoken gibberish before.* Again, some Scotch would have helped here. It was an incredibly awkward exercise as I tried to make up a new language while being spontaneous and creative. I wasn't feeling the divine flow, I wasn't able to put my brain on standby (curiously, that was an easy feat when I drove under the low bridge back in Winnipeg) and I was gripped by fears of looking like an incompetent non-actor.

My experience at improv mirrored the awkward feeling of my life in Nanaimo. I hadn't yet found that space where things flowed naturally. Some blocks still hindered me here and there and I was still living with some old familiar patterns. I hadn't yet found that space of complete fearlessness.

Both my improv and my life needed some work before feeling less gauche, but I left the workshop with a positive reminder. Good improv and good living share one key element in common; you have to learn to make the most out of what you have on hand.

~

I'd never seen so much rain before. I had actually considered getting *Miss Daisy* some pontoons or a really big lifejacket. A freakish rain and wind storm had left much of Nanaimo flooded and landlocked, as all ferries leaving the Island had been cancelled. I was to leave for Seattle that night, via ferry, for a much-needed trip to Florida, but my hopes and plans were quickly washed away by the storm.

The following morning I awoke to the sound of more rain pelting the roof of *Miss Daisy*. I felt like a lost soul, wondering why my heart had led me to this land of incessant rainfall and nightmarish haircuts.

That day, I felt the same way I did after taking some items from my former house to my tiny storage unit for the first time. As soon as I had returned to my house and walked in the door, I keeled over into tears. I recognized the feeling as it visited me again—the emotions were sitting close to the surface, poised at any moment to reveal themselves in tears, simply waiting for me to let them go.

I called my friend Tina and headed over to her Twilight Zone to commiserate about the monsoon rains and our alien existence on Planet Nanaimo. Like me, Tina had let go of a life in Ottawa that wasn't working out to find happiness somehow and somewhere else. We were soul mates in this rain-drenched, transformative and sometimes perplexing life experience.

Tina, a brilliant philosopher, summed up our situation with simple wisdom.

"We're caught in the in-between," she said. "We're at that place where we've let go of our past lives, but don't yet have a new life to grab onto." I understood and let my emotions sit uneasily with her comments.

My thoughts wandered back to a conversation we'd had at the improv workshop. While discussing patterns and clichés in life, Alan used the analogy of a paint-by-number kit versus the inspired artist who creates a masterpiece from the soul, using a blank canvas.

Many of us take a paint-by-number approach to our lives. I know that I certainly did. We're given a template of what the picture of our life should look like and we are even given the lines to paint within. We simply apply the colours and then stand back to look at our finished product, a painting that is actually not our own creation. When I stood back and examined my own paint-by-number picture, it didn't bear a resemblance to the masterpiece I'd imagined for my own life. It appeared rather lifeless and looking at it no longer brought me any joy.

My adventure with *Miss Daisy* was about erasing my paint-by-number piece. I needed to take away the colours, the shapes and remove the lines, so that I could start from scratch with a blank canvas. And it'd been a lot of work. It had taken quite some time to paint it in the first place.

It had taken all the months since selling my home, packing up my belongings and driving a Daisymobile all summer to begin to remove the paint. The emotions sitting close to the surface as I spoke to Tina told me that there were still a few spots of colour remaining on my canvas.

"How will you know when your journey is over?" Tina asked.

I thought for a moment.

"I'll know I am finished when I have a new painting before me. This part of my journey will be complete when I have a painting that is vibrant and exciting. It'll be a painting that I can share with the world and gladly call my own creation."

Feeling some resolve after my visit with Tina I headed home to *Miss Daisy*. As I had done once before, when I crossed the RV threshold, the tears began and continued until I'd completely fallen asleep. I was okay with them as they fell like drops of paint onto my pillow.

Awaking the next morning, my canvas felt completely blank. I was ready to begin a fresh painting.

chapter 38

Life felt sweeter. Nanaimo seemed sweeter too.

It is amazing the big difference that a small square can make.

chapter 39

Having the Island
Time of My Life

Miss Daisy was giving me the cold shoulder. Actually, she was giving me the cold everything.

It was an early December evening. My attire consisted of my winter jacket, toque and mittens, which is perfectly normal for that time of year. The problem was that I was wearing this outfit inside *Miss Daisy* where her core temperature had dropped to zero. I was shivering, my teeth chattering. Through my blue lips I muttered a few choice expletives. I was not a happy RV camper.

I'd been away for the weekend visiting my new friends, Roy and Bea, and had returned to receive a frosty reception from *Miss Daisy*. A small glacier had formed on my water supply outlet after my heat tape had failed, putting an end to running water. *Miss Daisy* was as warm as a meat locker on the inside since I'd turned off my heat while I was away.

Oh how I'd wished I'd asked my Mom to knit a giant sweater for *Miss Daisy*, then all this wouldn't have happened. Either that or my prolific knitting Mom could have sewn together the 1.2 million dish clothes she knit that year to make a lovely quilt. On a side note, if you'd like some colourful, hand-knit dish clothes, just let me know. I can hook you up.

It took a full day to thaw out *Miss Daisy*, my water supply lines and get her ready for winter. Thankfully, memories of a warm weekend with new friends melted away my frustration. While *Miss Daisy* and I had seen many beautiful parts of the country, it was always the people we met along the way that meant the most.

~

Bea was 75 and drove a purple Jeep outfitted in giant sunflowers and peace-loving bumper stickers. As you might imagine, I liked her immediately.

A former resident of Ottawa, she had emailed me over the summer after hearing about my travels via her daughter who lives in Ottawa. Bea mentioned that she lived on Salt Spring Island, a small island community not far from Nanaimo.

Her spunk was apparent in her initial message. She mentioned a long list of her community activities, including that she was a leading member of the Salt Spring Raging Grannies, a passionate group of activist women. Bea also volunteered at the library, cared for a 96-year-old friend, gardened, took care of her two dogs, and was happily married. We forged a quick friendship and corresponded frequently throughout the summer.

Someone once told me that many refer to Salt Spring Island as "a difference of opinions surrounded by water." Early that December, I decided to visit this curious island. Of course, I also wanted to meet Bea so I sent a message asking if she'd like to meet up for a cup of tea.

"You'll stay here with me and Roy (her husband)!" was her enthusiastic reply. I knew better than to attempt to say no to a feisty 75-year old.

I later learned that some folks thought it was strange or unwise of me to accept such an invitation from a relative stranger. Others found it strange of Bea and Roy to invite a relative stranger into their home for a weekend.

"You don't even know these people. Who the heck does this kind of thing?" remarked one of my friends. People who follow their heart do. I learned that you can have a heck of a good time when you make friends with strangers. And I also learned that the inhabitants of Salt Spring Island are indeed an opinionated lot.

~

I found an amazing soul connection with my new friends. After knowing Bea and Roy for 3.2 minutes, I'd felt I'd known them for a lifetime. We talked easily about our lives and I found Bea as spunky in person as her email suggested.

When I awoke Sunday morning, Bea was watching a news report about the Copenhagen Climate Summit at which Paul McCartney was delivering a few words.

"Sir Paul is looking good for his age," I remarked. Bea, who is a vegetarian, quipped, "That's because he's a vegetarian!" Even the carnivore in me appreciated her quick wit and suggestive commentary at 8 a.m. on a Sunday.

And, of course, I also loved the daisies on her Christmas stocking that was hung over the fireplace.

To discover that most of Bea's friends were 10 or 20 or 30 years her junior didn't surprise me. She's fervently young at heart and one needs a bit of an age handicap to keep up with her energy level. Although my 46 years to her 75 years matched us well in other ways too. We'd shared the same experiences in life but from different points of view—Bea as a mother, me as a daughter—the sharing of which seemed to deepen our bond even further.

In fact, I had such fun that my originally planned two-day visit extended itself into three and a half days. I couldn't resist an extra night's stay and the opportunity to attend Roy's inaugural music recital. With no shortage of spunk of his own, he'd just learned to play the trumpet at the age of 72.

On the final morning of my stay, I missed the ferry after being sidetracked into another captivating conversation with Bea.

Fortunately, I'd already been introduced to the concept of island time, the phenomenon whereby things just seem to take longer on an island.

Sure, my pipes had frozen while I was away, but new friends had warmed my heart and that made it all worthwhile.

~

I met Angie shortly after landing in Nanaimo. We'd first connected at a local women's business networking meeting where her positive, fun and engaging personality caught my attention. That and the fact that I learned she also enjoyed the occasional Nanaimo bar. A few days later we met up for a coffee and that was how our friendship began.

With Christmas approaching, Angie invited me to join her and her two kids on a road trip to visit a Christmas Village. Of course, I merrily said 'yes'.

When I arrived at Angie's house, a curiously large pile of carrots and vegetables greeted me at the front door. Angie welcomed me in and we quickly packed up the car for the drive. As we left she said, "Oh, don't let me forget to give you a bag of carrots before you leave. I'll tell you the story in the car."

I'll admit it, I was intrigued. I'd never been gifted carrots before. Our road trip to the Port Alberni Christmas Village would afford us more time to get acquainted and to find out the deal with the carrots. Our excursion also gave me a taste of the differences in the West Coast lifestyle.

It turns out that Angie's mom, who has five university degrees, is a small-plot intensive farmer who grows and sells organic vegetables, including carrots (and those were the best tasting carrots I'd ever had.) That's what people do on the island; they live and work their passion. They also share freely of themselves, a trait that I would argue is far less common in the big city.

Angie was also a transplant to Nanaimo, having moved with her husband Bruce six years prior to start their business. Having made major life changes myself, I loved her simple and clear perspective on change, big or small.

"It's just a decision," she said.

True. In the end, having what you truly want in life is just a decision about going for it or not.

It wouldn't have been another day on the island if we'd been on time. We arrived back in Nanaimo four hours later than originally planned. That was okay with me, I was having the island time of my life with my newfound friends.

chapter 40

My Christmas Gift

I approached that Christmas with hesitation. It would be the first time I'd spent Christmas away from my family in years. Not only that, but I'm one of the three people on the planet who truly love fruitcake and I'd be missing out on my Mom's decadent homemade version. I worried whether Christmas would leave me feeling very alone.

"You are exactly where you need to be," offered a wise friend. I knew he was right. I couldn't be disappointed or afraid. I was meant to be in Nanaimo, for whatever reason and that I would find out soon enough.

~

Much to my delight, it turned out to be a very special Christmas that year.

The festivities began at my friend Penny's where we enjoyed dinner and exchanged gifts. Penny gave me a magazine containing an article by Deepak Chopra on harnessing the power of 'synchrodestiny', the mysterious web of coincidences that guides us to fulfill our *dharma* or purpose in life. As someone who follows daisies and believes in the synchronicity of seemingly unconnected life events, I knew that even 'coincidentally' coming across such an article was nothing short of synchrodestiny at work. What was the message for me?

These words spoke directly to my heart:

"Your dharma is your destiny, the path of least resistance. It's the course that is most right and most nourishing—that brings you the greatest fulfillment and the most happiness.... Each of us has a gift, a special purpose that we alone can give to the world. And once we discover this gift, we've achieved our true purpose in life."

My heart tugged me to Westwood Lake, the perfect place for some serene reflection on these words. It was a crisp wintry evening as I stood by the side of the lake thinking about dharma.

"What do you do?" It was a question I'd struggled with in recent weeks and months whenever I was asked. If I responded truthfully and said, "I drive a Daisymobile and I always do the speed limit," dazed and confused looks generally followed. I've 'done' many things in life, from chef to fundraiser to shoe-fitting specialist to bed and breakfast owner. All of my career hats had fit nicely into some sort of box. Yet they'd all eventually reached the point where they didn't feel like a fit anymore. Perhaps I'd needed to travel the path of resistance on my way to discovering the path of least resistance.

It was a crisp and clear wintry night. The stars glistened and danced above, offering their own gift to the occasion. The full, bright moon took centre stage illuminating the water, the mountains, the surrounding trees and my own thoughts, as if to say, "And let there be light."

And there was.

I spoke to God, the universe, whomever was listening and I made my Christmas wish into a question. *What am I meant to do with my life?*

The answer came quickly.

It wasn't a big surprise. If I'd heard a loud voice bellowing from the heavens, "Heather, become an accountant," then I would have been surprised. The path of least resistance for me had simply involved following my heart wherever it took me—and helping others to do the same. A little nudge on my shoulder told me that was my dharma, my destiny in life, as unconventional as it may seem. What that would mean to my life or how that might unfold in career terms, I had no idea. I would leave those details to the higher powers.

Without question, the miracle of synchrodestiny had brought me to Westwood Lake that night. Otherwise, I may not have received the best Christmas gift of all, which was discovering the unique gift inside me.

chapter 41

Six Months Down the Road

My phone rang. It was Penny.

"What time will you be here on New Year's Day for the Polar Bear Dip?" she asked.

"Huh? When did I ever agree to such a thing?" I replied, shuddering at the thought of diving into the ocean on January 1st.

"I mentioned it to you back in September and you said you'd do it." *Yeah, Penny, that's like politely saying 'Sure, let's do lunch sometime' to someone you don't ever intend to have lunch with.*

I couldn't say no. Even though I prefer to avoid cold water, Penny had kindly welcomed me to Nanaimo with a Nanaimo bar after all.

On the morning of the New Year, Tina, Penny and I shored up our bravado by downing a couple of shots of warm rum. Then, sexily dressed in our long underwear, we headed to the beach for the group plunge at noon. *How do I get myself into these predicaments?*

The bullhorn sounded and 75 of us raced into the chilling waters of the Pacific Ocean. I didn't linger, opting to stay in only long enough to be able to claim the bragging rights to the experience. I'll share a little secret with you though. It wasn't as bad as I thought it would be. Much to my surprise, it was actually kind of fun. All the more so since my biggest fear, having a heart attack, did not come to fruition.

It was a refreshing way to begin the New Year and to celebrate six months of being on the road. I'd also hoped that it might jolt some new energy into the year ahead as some challenges had appeared on the horizon of 2010.

~

Originally, I'd only planned to be on the road for four months, but my heart wanted me to linger for longer. Extending my plan meant welcoming more changes and newness into life, more time away from my old friends, establishing a new life in Nanaimo and experiencing the side effects in my bank account.

While still rewarming myself after my New Year's Day dip, I reflected back on the past half year and took a brief inventory.

I felt happy to have sold my house and found a way to do something I'd always wanted to do. I loved my new, simplified life with fewer possessions and worries. I felt spiritually alive and free, more in tune with myself and my true life path. I felt a comfort I'd not felt before in life. I felt stronger and more confident, having ventured on my own. I was richer and I was poorer. The adventure had also cost me much more than I'd imagined it would.

I recalled the feeling I had when I left Ottawa, that life was somehow divinely guiding me towards my destiny. I had trusted that my crazy daisy experience would eventually lead to the place of finding myself and creating the life of my dreams.

Many folks along the way had told me that they would like to take a similar journey, perhaps not in an RV, but one of their own design. They'd like to let set themselves free from the shackles of their lives but feel that they can't. Work, finances, family, house, time or relationships usually top their list of reasons why.

I'd contend that most folks are simply afraid. They're afraid to follow the call of their heart and do what they really want because it would mean change. It could mean huge change. It would mean risk. It would mean uncertainty. It could mean financial costs. It might mean that they lose friends, colleagues or relationships. It would mean that things would be very different.

I'd contend that that is the whole point. Follow your heart so that life will be different.

So many people are struggling in fear in a life that isn't bringing them happiness. With each day, their spirits are slowly dying.

I often wonder how different our world would be if everyone lived the life they truly wanted. If everyone's heart was alive with joy and passion. I wonder what it would be like if more people could choose faith instead of fear.

I'd simply reached the point where I was no longer afraid of letting go of what I had and what I knew. I was far more afraid of never uncovering what was calling me from within or never experiencing the kind of life that I truly wanted.

That's what kept me going, the possibility of having a better life than the one I'd left behind.

As I looked ahead to 2010 and the uncertainties that lay ahead, strangely, I felt fine. I had to trust that life wouldn't have nudged me on this adventure without also safeguarding my path.

I must admit, however, that I was beginning to get concerned about my dwindling bank account.

~

Like everyone else who asked, you're probably wondering how I was able to finance my adventure. I was always intrigued by the assumptions that people would make.

"Did you save for years?" *No.*

"Are you retired?" *Absolutely not.*

And my personal favourite, "Gee, I'd love to have your bank account!" *No problem, I'll trade you for yours as it's likely much bigger than mine.*

There was not an unlimited supply of money in my bank account nor did I have a secret stash under my mattress.

At the time that I'd put my house up for sale, my financial picture was not pretty. I had been living beyond my means, juggling two businesses and a part-time job to try to make ends meet. Over a period of six years, I had accumulated a great deal of debt trying to maintain my house and my lifestyle, which was not extravagant by any means. I know that I am not alone in having fallen into the debt trap. By spring 2009, my credit cards were maxed out, one credit card company had put a lien against my house and I was also behind on several mortgage payments.

From the proceeds of the sale of my house, I was able to pay off all my debts. I was left with a five-figure sum with which to purchase *Miss Daisy* and finance my adventure.

There are some who will question how I landed in such a predicament. There are some who will question my decision to venture off in life without a source of income and a limited bank account that, by January 2010, was quite depleted.

I know this for sure. Life is what it is. Things are neither good nor bad. The situations that we find ourselves in are merely opportunities to learn, grow, to do things differently and perhaps, most importantly, to also help others along the way.

Leaving on my adventure didn't feel like a choice. Instead, the tug to go was so strong that it felt as if life had chosen it for me. I had to continue to trust that tug.

My faith was surely being tested that January. My financial picture was not looking bright and I didn't know what life would bring in the coming weeks and months. It was downright scary in fact. I was dining on oatmeal and Kraft Dinner on an all-too-regular basis. In a town with a very high unemployment rate, finding even a part-time job was proving to be very difficult.

I took a few deep breaths at the beginning of the year and tried to have faith. *Heather, life has always provided for you.* I also remembered my friend Santiago who had given up everything he had in pursuit of his dreams and had often teetered on the financial edge.

This test of faith was simply part of my journey of the heart. It would also be just one of the many tests that 2010 had in store for me in the coming months.

chapter 42

Julie and Julia and Heather

"You'll love it! It's totally you." Approximately 347 people had suggested that I needed to see the movie *Julie and Julia*. Hey, I know when life is trying to send me a message so I rented the movie one evening and watched it with a friend.

Julie and Julia tells the story of Julie Powell, a woman who spent a year cooking her way through Julia Child's *Mastering the Art of French Cooking*. She had meticulously documented her entire journey on her blog. The movie also follows the early stages of Julia Child's career, the years during which she wrote her acclaimed gastronomic masterpiece.

As a former professional chef, blogger and aspiring writer, I could relate to their stories from many perspectives. Perhaps more importantly, *Julie and Julia* came into my life as beacons at a time when doubt had entered my life. *Why did I uproot my life to venture off in a Daisymobile?*

I didn't know who to ask for advice so I looked to *Julie and Julia* for some answers. They seemed like soul sisters who'd both followed their heart in the pursuit of their dreams too.

We'd all started from the same place. Each of us had an inexplicable and undeniable yearning to do something, which may have seemed senseless, purposeless, impossible, irresponsible or futile to anyone but ourselves. Driven by a passion that came from deep within, we kept going not knowing how or when it would end.

Julie's pursuit was admirable. She prepared one or more of the classical French cuisine recipes from Julia Child's cookbook every day for an entire year. I know of people who've been driven to the brink of insanity just trying to cook the Thanksgiving turkey. Whereas she was holding down a full-time job while doing all of this cooking. Imagine spending a few hours preparing Mousse de Foies de Volaille, Homard à L'Americaine and Tarte au Citron et Aux Amandes after a long day at the office!

It was Julie's passion and it was simply something she felt compelled to do. Julie's story had a very happy and inspiring ending indeed. She published a book about her experience, which was later released as the aforementioned movie, and then continued her career as a writer.

It took eight years for Julia Child to write and publish her renowned tome of French cookery! Eight years! She wasn't immune to challenges along the way either. After her book was rejected by one publisher, she embarked upon a complete rewrite of the 720-page tome. It was eventually published and Ms. Child went on to enjoy a huge television and public career, inspiring and endearing millions around the world.

I felt inspired by both Julie and Julia. They were two soul sisters who had spent many hours toiling at their passions, simply driven by the excitement of doing it. Many may have called their pursuits 'purposeless', however, in the end they turned out to be divinely purposeful.

I had to believe that there was also a greater purpose to my endeavour as well.

~

"Why are you doing this?" I'd been asked that question many times by people trying to understand what would ever cause me to leave behind my comfortable life and take a drive of faith in a Daisymobile. They'd nod politely as I shared my thoughts and my dreams.

"Do you really think that's going to happen?" they'd ask.

I can only hypothesize that from their point of view my journey seemed pointless and without purpose. They didn't see a tangible end point. I couldn't see one either, I just kept putting one foot in front of the other because it felt like the most right thing I'd ever done in my life.

I simply wanted to see where following my heart would take me. It may not have made sense to some, but it made perfect sense to me. I'm sure there were moments when both Julie and Julia questioned their journey. I'm sure there were times when they had to dig deep to find the strength to keep going. I'm sure that they'd shed some tears along the way too.

Keep going Heather, just keep going. Julie and Julia offered me some much-needed encouragement at a time of questioning when things had begun to get very challenging.

Okay ladies, I will. If you can do it, so can I.

chapter 43

Great Things Happen When You Have Faith

I glanced at the subject line in my thread of emails that morning.

"Great things happen when you have faith." It was a fortuitous message on what I considered the worst day of my trip. I was beginning to discover that following your heart is not always an easy or fun thing to do.

I hadn't stayed in bed for an entire day since my days in the womb. On that particular day though, I stayed in bed, in my pyjamas, all day long. I was feeling seriously downtrodden.

Box of tissues in hand, I cried my way from morning until night as I stared into the void of the unknown that lay ahead of me. The sound of raindrops hitting the roof serenaded me throughout the day.

I must have been quite the sight. I was in dire need of a haircut and looked a little Einsteinesque. I couldn't afford one though as my bank account was rapidly bottoming out and I had no income on the horizon. To add to my economic misery, my SUV was in need of extensive repairs. The muffler wasn't muffling much of anything anymore and it had begun to sound like a low-flying aircraft as I drove around town. The rain continued to fall and *Miss Daisy* had mysteriously sprung a leak around her entrance door. It was cold day in the middle of January. I didn't know how I was going to pay my next month's rent at the RV park.

I was also out of Nanaimo bars. Things were truly bleak.

In between tears and thoughts of giving up on the pursuit of my dreams, I asked my heart for some guidance. *Um, okay so what do I do now?* No answer came. *Okey dokey then.* I was stumped.

I know that those who dare to pursue their dreams will face challenges along the way. It's simply the universe's way of testing you. How deeply are you committed to your dreams? Have you mastered the lessons along the way? How strong is your faith that you are being divinely guided on your path?

I was feeling very tested. I had taken huge risks, made big leaps and given up so much financially, emotionally, spiritually, personally and materially to reach this point. And I still didn't know what the path ahead might look like. On that particular day it was looking rather grim. But could I really give up on the dreams that I'd invested my heart and soul into? Would I give up or would I discover the faith I needed to keep moving forward into the unknown?

I called my friend Tara for a few words of encouragement. I shared and vented as tears flooded down my cheeks. When I was finished,

Tara calmly said, "Don't worry hon', this too shall pass." Somehow, I knew she was right.

Tara also pointed out a gift that I'd overlooked in the midst of my state of overwhelm. I had been asking my heart for some guidance. I had indeed received a very helpful reply that very morning.

Great things happen when you have faith.

chapter 44

Into Every Life a Little Rain Must Fall

I'd just surpassed the six-month mark. That would explain why I was teetering on the verge of insanity most days.

I'd just returned from dinner with a friend who'd also lived in her RV for several months when she first relocated to Nanaimo. She, too, had enjoyed the initial excitement of living in her rig in a quaint RV park by the water. My friend also knowingly spoke about the threshold point, the point at which the charm of living in a space the size of a large walk-in closet begins to wear off. I had reached that threshold point and was slowing beginning to go stir crazy. The non-stop onslaught of rain only dampened the situation even further.

In sexy real estate marketing terms, my living space could have been described as "charmingly small, with everything at your fingertips." For someone on a journey of self-exploration it can be both a blessing and a curse. Everywhere you turn there you are. You cannot get away from yourself. "Enjoy this time because you'll come to appreciate it. It'll never happen again," my friend kindly suggested. *I may be very thankful if it doesn't.*

~

I didn't know that so much rain could fall from the sky. Coming from an area of Canada that is well-known for its snowy and cold winters, this was a difficult adjustment for me.

"You need to find something to keep you from going insane over the winter," advised a fellow I chatted with at the local hot tub. I wondered if I was already too far gone to be brought back to the land of the sunny disposition.

When I first arrived in Nanaimo, I'd noticed many shops advertising vitamin D supplements. At the same time, I'd noticed many shops selling Nanaimo bars and opted to supplement myself with those instead. In hindsight, that may have been a mistake. While I was high in vitamin Nanaimo bar I may have been dangerously low in vitamin sunshine.

As the saying goes, into every life a little (or a lot of) rain must fall. Evidently my life called for a monsoon. I certainly appreciated the sunshine when it came to visit, which lasted approximately seven minutes for the entire month of January.

Sometimes when we have too much of a good thing, we don't notice it as much nor appreciate it any more. Sometimes we also need to step away from what we had to see what was lacking.

Certainly life in Ottawa had more sunshine. I also had good friends and a network there. I had a house with a roof that didn't leak and I had an income. There weren't mountains and an ocean there however. Ottawa didn't offer the laid-back lifestyle and it no longer made my heart sing the way that the West Coast did.

Contrast brings appreciation. And perspective. And growth.

Hmmm. Maybe I spiritually needed the rain. Maybe that's why it seemed as if life was pelting me with monsoon rain and monsoon challenges.

I needed to be uncomfortable, apparently very uncomfortable, to find the joy and gratitude in my experience. Yes, it rained a lot in a Nanaimo winter, but when the sun did shine, it was incredibly beautiful. Yes, my life was full of challenges that January, but I was alive, following my dreams and I had so much Self to be proud of.

I'll admit that it would take a while longer for me to get fully comfortable with the amount of rain in my Nanaimo life. Still, I had found glimmers of sunshine in my world. And for that, I had the rain to be thankful for.

chapter 45

Test #147 of Faith

It is often said that God never gives you more than you can handle. It appeared that God thinks that I can handle a lot.

It had been pouring rain for days and my mood had become as grey as the skies. Darkness also reigned inside the confined space of *Miss Daisy* and RV living had become as appealing as having all my teeth removed without anaesthetic.

My normally upbeat and positive self was nowhere to be found. In her place was a somewhat despondent woman battling an army of stressors that was launching ongoing emotional, spiritual, environmental, physical, and financial attacks.

My mood and spirit were incredibly low. No matter how I tried, I couldn't seem to dig them out of the hole they had fallen into. I felt immobilized, depressed, scared and alone as I stared into the nothingness before me. *This isn't fun anymore.*

I was tired of having rain visit every day. I couldn't find the joy in it anymore. My living quarters were small, dingy, damp and cold. I missed the snow of Eastern Canada.

My finances were running dangerously low. A recent synchronous set of circumstances led to the sale of my SUV, which gave me enough cash to cover some bills and buy some food. I now had $30 left in my bank account and had miraculously been able to make it through the past week on only $6. Still, I didn't have enough money to pay my next month's rent at the RV park.

It's always good to try to find the bright side if you can. I was eating less, walking more and my pants felt looser. That was my tiny ray of sunshine in the midst of it all.

I'd just spoken to my friend Pat about the hardships I was facing as I grasped at any straw that I could to diminish my pain. Her advice was to accept where I was as part of the bigger picture. My problem was that I didn't want to stand in my 'now' because it kind of sucked. It was hard to get excited about my 'now' when it often included having oatmeal for dinner. It felt much easier said than done to get into my 'now', particularly since my 'now' involved a large degree of discomfort and uncertainty.

I headed to the lake to have a conversation with the folks up above and see what they might have to say. *Hi there, it's me again, the one in the Daisymobile. What do I do next? I'm scared and not having fun anymore. Please help me.*

I patiently waited for the answer. It came to me as a loud silence.

The answer was simply that I needed to have faith. Coincidentally, I was in a situation where it was nearly the only thing I had left.

Life seemed to be putting my beliefs and my faith to the test.

Until that point, it'd been easy to believe. I had had some sense of security, some thing to hold onto. It was easy to believe when I had a full bank account, plenty of food in the fridge and few challenges coming my way. I could stand safely by the shore and imagine the possibilities out at sea.

I hadn't truly experienced the meaning of faith.

I was far from shore with my empty bank account, limited food supply and many challenges in my way. My former sense of security was nowhere to be found.

I needed to find my faith. And I guess that God figured I was up for the challenge. I took a few deep breaths.

Okay God. I let all my troubles go and hand things over to you. Surely you can do a better job at things than I can. I don't have to worry anymore because I know that you're by my side.

My heart was quiet, telling me not to worry. Maybe it was telling me to have faith. *Heather, 'now' is the perfect time to start having faith. In fact, the best time to learn faith is 'now'.*

chapter 46

On the Road Again

My mother would not be thrilled, but at least Lao Tzu would have approved of my most recent change in plans. These words landed with divine timing in my email inbox on the morning of February 1, the day that I moved out of the RV park. It summed up my situation beautifully for I had no fixed plans and once again, no fixed address.

I had packed up my campsite and said goodbye to what had been my home by Westwood Lake. I simply did not have enough money to pay the rent anymore. A mix of trepidation and nervous excitement greeted me as I prepared to drive away from campsite #42. I was quasi-homeless, with very little money and would be living without heat and running water in the middle of the winter. This wasn't exactly the scenario that I would have imagined for myself. At the same time, I felt a sense of adventure about the experience.

I felt as though it was part of a greater whole, a whole that was in my heart.

~

When I had first arrived at Westwood Lake and set up camp with *Miss Daisy*, I looked forward to some respite from nearly six months of a nomadic lifestyle. I longed for the basic securities in life such as knowing where I'd be every day, where to do laundry, where to shower and where to buy Nanaimo bars. Feeling somewhat settled and comfortable was appealing to me after several months on the road.

The first month brought the Man Cut, monsoon rain and being lost nearly every time I went out on the town. The second month brought slightly more familiarity, some new friends and the holiday season. The third month, January, brought more rain and clouds, some challenges and an overall lack of fun in life. A way of life that I'd thought would be comfortable became entirely uncomfortable in many ways. In fact, life felt stagnant.

Not being able to pay the rent may have been the blessing that I needed. I missed movement, I missed the freedom and adventure of being on the road and I missed driving *Miss Daisy*. I don't think that she liked it at Westwood Lake either. She was the kind of RV who was meant to be out on the road, wind in her daisies, driving along the open highway sharing her daisy love.

Any trepidation I had about leaving my campsite melted away the moment I popped my Doobie Brothers' tape into the cassette deck. I cranked *Miss Daisy's* engine, cranked up *Listen to the Music* and drove away from Westwood Lake with absolutely no idea where I was going.

Lao Tzu would have been impressed. My mother would not.

~

For my first night on the road, I returned to where it had all began in Nanaimo, the glamorous Walmart parking lot. As I'd done that first night after arriving in Nanaimo, I parked *Miss Daisy* and headed out for a walk by the ocean. Some people cast their wishes upon a star. I cast mine amongst the natural divinity of the island surroundings. In spite of my circumstances, I continued to believe in my bigger goals and dreams in life. I continued to believe that somehow this crazy journey I was on would eventually take me to them.

I looked to the ocean, the mountains and the sky. *My life may look a bit crazy at the moment but this is what I eventually see for myself. I see myself becoming a successful published author and public speaker. I see myself helping people around the world. I see myself having a home again someday. I see that home being on Vancouver Island. I see myself connecting with my soul mate. I see myself having a life that I love. I trust that You, the powers of the universe, and my heart will help me create this new life. Thank you.*

And with that, my wish list was in. I had no idea how any of it might manifest, I only had faith that somehow it would.

Just moments later, an eagle flew overhead. I took it as a good sign and a message from above. My prayers had been heard.

~

"This is hilarious," I said to Tina. She'd met me for a coffee at Starbucks that first night. I'd just settled into my new digs and we held what was more of a Walmart-warming party than your traditional housewarming event.

We both laughed and nodded in disbelief at my arrangement.

"I'm 46 years old, it's February and I'm living in my RV in the parking lot at Walmart. When will I ever be able to say this again?" I said. *Well, hopefully it would only happen once but you never know.*

You may as well as embrace the adventure whatever it looks like when it enters your life. It wasn't that bad. I received a friendly welcome every time I walked in the door at Walmart to use the washroom. Free internet and electricity could be found only a two-minute walk away at Starbucks. If I didn't like my neighbours, I could just pick up and move my rig.

I was no longer hooked up to power or running water however. Luckily, the nearby RV dump station offered a fresh water supply and I enjoyed warm showers and a hot tub at the local recreation centre.

My generator seemed to be on a long winter's nap from which it did not want to be awakened. This meant that I didn't have power, even on a short-term basis, and more importantly, I did not have heat.

It might have been nice to have been experiencing nightly hot flashes at the time but I wasn't. I slept in all my clothes and my ski jacket that first night. It was a chilly winter's evening.

My life appeared somewhat abnormal, yet I felt strangely re-energized and reconnected to my purpose again. Maybe some change and new discomfort was the shake-up that I needed to move forward, somehow. It was a new and exciting adventure, challenges and all.

I would certainly have the opportunity to understand deeply what it means to trust life and to follow your heart. That was my ultimate destination and what I'd signed up for when I left on this gig.

In my favour was the fact that I was not intent on arriving on any set schedule. I wanted to be a good traveller after all.

chapter 47

Expecting the Unexpectations

I hadn't expected the unexpected. You may find that silly on my part considering the number of times we're told in life to expect them, these unexpected things. I suppose that I was simply too busy following my heart to consider them.

Expect the unexpected. It's a nice thought that is well-intended to help one plan for unexpected variables ahead. We often don't know what the unexpected variables may be however, until they're staring us in the face. And only then are we able to figure out what to do about them.

I wonder what my response would have been if someone had asked me before I left on my trip: "Heather, what are you going to do if you end up extending your trip, land on a rainy island in the middle of winter, get depressed, can't find a job, run out of money and end up living at Walmart in February without running water, heat or electricity?" *Hmm, let me ponder that and get back to you. I don't have a frigging clue!* If I'd known that all that would happen, I never would have left Ottawa in the first place.

I hadn't expected many of the unexpected things that had happened along the way. I also hadn't expected that my own expectations would be one of my biggest challenges.

It's human nature to want life to be easy and relatively challenge-free. Witness rush hour traffic in any major city and it's clear that most folks get anxious when their road ahead is blocked. Most of us also like icing on our cake so we'd like to know what's coming around the next corner in life. Many of us even expect things to happen a certain way. *But there's always been chocolate icing on my cake before!* If things don't happen the way we'd expected, disappointment quickly follows.

I'd arrived in Nanaimo with some expectations of my own. After a wonderful summer of travel with *Miss Daisy*, I thought the transition would be easy. I thought that the fun would continue, that my hair would be perfect, and that everything would come up daisies.

I had not considered the fact that anyone who takes their ship of dreams out of safe harbour and heads off into the ocean is likely to encounter some stormy waters along the way.

My arrival in Nanaimo had greeted me with stormy waters indeed. Despite the ready availability of authentic Nanaimo bars at every turn, I often questioned my decision to winter in Nanaimo. I'd had no success finding even part-time work, I didn't have a large network of friends to lean on and I often felt depressed. I wasn't having fun anymore. I was not the life of the party. In fact, I frequently felt alone for the first time and somewhat of a lost soul.

I had hoped and perhaps expected that January would mark a fresh start. Instead, along came the unexpected. Many tears, feelings of being stuck, more rain, frustration, moments of lost hope and faith, anxiety in the midst of uncertainty, emotions that needed to be healed, questioning and doubt … all took turns haunting my days.

I had landed in some sort of very dark place of depression or despair, but it was the unexpected that I hadn't expected. I'll admit that initially I was angry about it. I resented it. This was supposed to be my fun, mid-life adventure, why did I have to face all these challenges? Was it really necessary?

Yes. It was.

~

I felt relieved to wake up one morning to see bright sunshine and hear the birdsong of spring. A shift had finally happened.

Over the past few weeks, I'd been battling my haunters. Finally, it seemed that I was slowly winning the battle to banish them from my life.

Gratitude had replaced my anger towards the darkness that had come to visit. I had come to appreciate the unexpected.

Winter had eventually turned to spring. Sunshine had finally replaced the rain.

I had shed many tears but had come to notice new joy. Faith and I had become closer because our friendship had been greatly tested. My previous fears had left town. I experienced and therefore I learned. I became resourceful and found strengths I didn't know that I had. Pain and discomfort will do that to you. Uncertainty now meant possibility. I valued simple things like heat, hydro and water, and didn't take them for granted anymore. Simple things brought me great happiness. I wondered why I'd worried about anything because my worrying hadn't changed a thing.

I'd faced some big challenges and they hadn't killed me. Maybe they weren't really that big after all.

Now I wouldn't have expected to hear myself say that a few weeks ago. But then again, I had never expected the unexpected.

chapter 48

You Can't Rush a Journey

Flowers were in bloom, the sun was shining, the air was warm. March had arrived. I had spent the winter on Vancouver Island.

It was time to think about what was next.

For some reason, Ottawa quietly called my name. I wasn't sure that I saw myself living there permanently again. Maybe I simply missed my friends. I wondered whether I could ever be happy living there again.

Nanaimo called my name too. I enjoyed the West Coast lifestyle, a slower-paced existence set against the backdrop of the ocean and the mountains. I loved Nanaimo bars. I wondered whether I'd be happier starting over in Nanaimo and making an entirely new life for myself.

Did I dare to dream about the possibility of someday having a home in both cities? I wanted the best of both worlds; comfort and familiarity of good friends on one hand and a place of new adventures and unparalleled beauty on the other.

I also wondered about what to do with *Miss Daisy*. It had been nine months and I'd begun to grow tired of living in my 100 square feet of living space. The upkeep and the expense of keeping *Miss Daisy* in the lifestyle to which she'd become accustomed was also becoming daunting. I longed for a fixed address of some sort, with basics like heat, hydro and running water. Those had become precious luxuries in life while I was roving around on the streets of Nanaimo. Should I drive *Miss Daisy* back to Ottawa for one last fling on the road? Or should I sell her?

There was much to wonder about, including how life would pan out with the tiny new addition to the Daisy family now on board.

~

She was all of four pounds, but what she lacked in weight she certainly made up for in attitude. Jack Russell Terriers are like that, well-known for their feisty Napoleonic personalities. I named my new puppy Daisy Nanaimo Bar after two of my favourite things in life. Most of the time I just call her Daisy 'Mo.

She brought a doggie breath of fresh air into my world. I'd been on my own for a long time, it was nice to have a travelling companion for a change. Even one that launched regular attacks on my ankles and pant legs with her sharp, puppy teeth.

Daisy 'Mo's presence certainly helped take my mind off big life issues like where to live and how to pay for things. I was kept far too busy trying to stop her from stealing my socks, chewing the inside of *Miss Daisy* or breaking out of her crate with the skill and finesse of

Houdini.

The first time it happened, I'd gone to Starbucks for an hour. I'd left Daisy 'Mo safely in her crate, with the door firmly closed. So I thought.

Upon my return to *Miss Daisy*, the sight of Daisy 'Mo running around with her head stuck inside my jar of peanut butter greeted me as I walked through the door.

The next morning I double-checked the latch on the crate door before I hit the road for a drive downtown. *Yep, it's shut tight!* So I thought.

Only minutes later, as I drove along the highway, a certain exuberantly happy white puppy jumped up on the dashboard. I guess she wasn't pleased with the view from her crate and decided to make a dash for something better, literally. From her vantage point on the dash, Daisy 'Mo stared me right in the face as if to say, "Oh yeah, you think you can keep me in that thing while you drive?" At 90 kilometres per hour, I couldn't argue her point.

After it happened the third time, I realized that serious measures would be called for. During the third breakout, I'd lost an entire package of Fig Newton's. That also meant that I lost an entire night's sleep taking a very fibre-filled puppy out for hourly bathroom breaks. After that incident, I got wiser. Three carabiners now helped secure the door in Hannibal Lector fashion.

I think she retaliated by biting my ankles even harder after that.

~

I was at another transition point. I had spent my winter in Nanaimo as I'd planned but I still didn't know what I was going to do next. I was 'in between' again and it was an uncomfortable place to be.

"What do I do now? What do I really want?" I asked myself those questions on a regular basis and couldn't get a clear answer.

I asked the universe for some sort of direction. In short order, I received several mixed messages from helpful friends who kindly offered their advice.

"Heather, I think you need to head back to Ottawa and set up home there." Another suggested, "Heather, I think you need to make a commitment to Nanaimo for six months." Yet another said, "I think you're still on a journey and just need to trust that." I may as well have asked the Three Little Bears for advice.

My patience was dearly being tested as I wanted some sort of answer.

Although, in many ways, my patience was being tested far more by having to train and share my wee RV space with a feisty terrier.

As my friend Tara often says, "Life doesn't give you what you want, it gives you what you need."

I wanted an answer. Life and Daisy 'Mo were both teaching me to practice patience. Perhaps that was exactly what I needed.

~

Maybe I was still on a journey and not ready to make any big decisions. It was certainly apparent that I wasn't ready to make long-term plans.

"So where are you parked right now?" asked an acquaintance I ran into at the pub one night.

"I'm parked downtown," I replied.

"Where are you going to park for the summer?" she asked.

"Park for the summer? I don't even know what I'm doing next week."

There was a pregnant pause. Make that a pregnant elephant pause as her investment planner brain tried to wrap itself around the idea of my lack of plans. She turned white as a ghost and disappeared from our conversation as quickly as one too.

No, I didn't have a long term plan. I hadn't even thought further than dessert. I wasn't 'there' yet, at that place of 'knowing' where I was headed next.

It's a bit like standing in line at the grocery, you can't rush your way to the checkout. You'll get there when you get there.

The challenge is trying to enjoy the wait in line.

During a recent conversation, my good friend Lynn shared a remarkable story of one of her adventures in life. She'd once lived in the backwoods of British Columbia in a plastic shelter she'd built with her husband. It was a basic shelter that they'd constructed of 2 X 4 wood beams and heavy sheets of plastic. They had even somehow rigged up a stove and a pump for water. They lived this unconventional lifestyle in the midst of nature for a few years. Lynn had even given birth to one of their daughters in their plastic home, without so much as a midwife present! She still maintains that those days remain amongst the fondest of her life.

Her story got me thinking. Perhaps I was in the midst of one of the best times of my life too, hardships, uncertainty and all.

I didn't need to rush to make any plans or any type of decision. You can't rush a grocery line. You can't rush a journey either.

I was still in a dazed state, with a good-size bump on my head and numbness in my arm and shoulder.

Lifeguards rushed in and walked me to a nearby bench to recover. My mind flashed back to some decadent dining I'd enjoyed the past few days when my sister came to visit. Fish and chips, Greek food, Mexican food, Nanaimo bars … I wondered whether I'd had a stroke in the aftermath of such indulgence.

If this is my day to go, at least I've lived life the way I wanted to. And I got to enjoy some good food and one last hot tub outing on the way out too. I thought that Fred would have been impressed.

The paramedics quickly determined that I hadn't had a stroke. I'd just stayed in the hot tub too long and had over-poached myself.

Thanks to Fred, I'd actually had a near-life experience. I was a few words of wisdom closer to living the kind of life that I truly wanted, one that made sense for me and one that just felt right.

And someday, any day, just like Fred, I'd be able to glance back and say, "Yeah, that was a good life."

chapter 50

Easter Renewal

Good Friday could have been renamed 'An Incredibly Blustery Day'
as Nanaimo was hit by power outages, more monsoon rain and
winds that rocked *Miss Daisy* from side to side as I attempted to
sleep. I had visions of *Miss Daisy* rolling across the Walmart parking
lot like a wayward tumbleweed. Although it could have been the
freezing cold that had kept me awake too. Either way, I was under-
slept and over-grumpy.

I'd been looking forward to a weekend of renewal and rejuvenation.
As I turned the pages on the calendar to welcome spring, I was faced
with the realization that it had been nearly one year since I'd sold
my house. A year later I still felt in between homes, not yet firmly
planted in Nanaimo nor having left Ottawa entirely behind either.

Life still didn't seem to be flowing for me and I was hoping that
some answers might appear. I was fatiguing of life in *Miss Daisy*. I
still had no income in sight. I continued to feel a slight tug in the
direction of Ottawa, but had no idea how I could afford a trip east.
Many things still felt uncertain.

Tina, my closest friend in Nanaimo, had just left town, headed back
to Ottawa for a month or more to help pack up the family home.

Her departure had left me feeling uneasy as she was a familiar friend to me, someone I could count on for support and understanding.

Life has a peculiar balancing act however. Just as Tina left, I received an email from a woman named Trish who'd also moved to the West Coast from Ottawa. We shared a mutual friend back East who suggested that Trish and I get in touch. Trish had embarked on her own intriguing life journey and seemed a like-minded spirit. I was thrilled to be meeting her on Easter Sunday, thankful for the divine gift of another friend who shared an Ottawa connection.

These small details had big value, especially during difficult times. A few other positive events transpired later that week that, by my new standards, were somewhat noteworthy. I got to enjoy a mini-vacation, sort of, and dinner out, sort of.

~

When you're low on funds, it's time to get creative. So as a way to generate a few dollars, I decided to rent *Miss Daisy* to interested travellers.

I'd just completed a four-day rental, which had landed me enough money to buy some food outside of the oatmeal family and to pay a few bills. Thank you Easter Bunny or whomever helped out with the details.

A lovely Australian couple had rented *Miss Daisy* to go Tofino, the most westerly point on Vancouver Island and home to gorgeous beaches.

"Awesome rig mate!" was their reaction the first time they saw *Miss Daisy*.

"You'll keep my awesome rig on the right side of the road, yeah?" was the first thing I said upon hearing their Aussie accents. Memories of the meandering Australians I'd met back in Jasper flashed back into my mind.

I had yet to visit Tofino, but was happy that *Miss Daisy* would have a fun road trip. I felt even happier that she was helping generate a bit of cash for the Daisy family considering the operational drain she'd been the past few months. Thankfully, the Aussies hadn't crossed any yellow lines and the story had a happy ending for all. They were thrilled with their trip, particularly since the local campsite manager in Tofino had offered them a free stay simply because he dug *Miss Daisy's* flowery vibe.

With *Miss Daisy* out of town, I was left to find a temporary home for myself and Daisy 'Mo. Luxury is in the eye of the beholder I would say. After a few months without regular access to running water or hydro, a few nights in a local low-budget motel felt quite glamorous. Our room was basic, but it wasn't like I was on my honeymoon. Thank God.

The roof didn't leak and I could have a hot shower or watch TV whenever I wanted. Thanks to our central location next to the Kentucky Fried Chicken outlet, I even enjoyed a finger lickin' good dinner outing one evening.

It was royal experience indeed. I felt like a friggin' Queen.

But I was all too soon back to my usual routine at Walmart while dearly hopeful that some clarity would come during the season of renewal.

To aid in that process, I decided to spring clean *Miss Daisy* with as much vigour as the storm that was swirling outside. I cleaned, sorted and purged, hoping that a shift of any sort would be helpful to my overall life feng shui.

With winter now behind me, it seemed time to remove the insulation I'd put over my rear windows in an attempt to keep my sleeping quarters warm. As I did, brilliant light poured in the windows. *Wow, I hadn't realized how much darker the space had become after I'd added the insulation.*

I felt better already. The darkness had lifted and some light had finally been shed onto my life after all.

chapter 51

The Power of the Flower

Maybe I'd been looking at it all the wrong way.

I'd spent much time in recent weeks pondering my next steps in life and wanting to make them happen somehow. I had been looking around my life and saw worry, an empty wallet, a small RV, a busy puppy, and many question marks. A little voice whispered to me one day, reminding me of something I'd once read. It was a passage about how to find greater inner strength. *Stop being so focused on yourself and start asking how you can best serve others.*

The words echoed through me. I had lost sight of the bigger picture.

Preoccupied with my own troubles, I'd forgotten my purpose. Yes, I wanted to follow my heart but more than that, I wanted to share my experiences and lessons learned along the way with others. Maybe the challenges of the recent weeks and months were as much a part of my purpose as the good times.

Certainly there was no fooling with the events that unfolded on April 1. They left me with no doubt that I was exactly where I was meant to be, doing exactly what I was meant to be doing.

I still smile and shake my head in stunned disbelief. But hey, that's the power of a daisy.

~

I had an entirely innocuous start to my April 1. A trip to the local mall, a few errands and then I returned to *Miss Daisy*. A rather significant debate as to whether to drive downtown to the gym or back to Walmart ensued. My Libra brain, which has the endearing ability to make painfully slow decisions, volleyed the decision ball back and forth for quite some time. Thankfully, some intuitive sense took hold of the situation like a SWAT team and told me to return to Walmart.

I obeyed and shortly after my arrival at the retail mecca, I left *Miss Daisy* to walk to a nearby coffee shop to meet a friend. While waiting for my friend, I received an email on my Blackberry, with the subject line, "You Touched Me Today."

At first, I thought it was a joke until I read further.

"I was feeling a bit melancholy today as it would have been my dear, much missed, mother-in-law's birthday if she was still alive. Her name was Daisy. I came out of Walmart to get in my truck and there shining in front of the grey sky was your motor home with the daisies all over. I had to stop and take a picture with my phone and send it to her other two kids as I know they will get a kick out of it too. We always say she is still with us and I think she must have put you there at that time to cheer me up. Admire your gumption and will visit your blog periodically. Keep on keepin' on."

I'd had many interesting coincidences and synchronicities while adventuring around in *Miss Daisy*, but this one took the proverbial cake. Or in my case, the proverbial Nanaimo bar.

I returned Jane's kind and heartfelt email, noting what was clearly a divine act of intervention that day, the lift that both of our hearts needed. While seeing *Miss Daisy* had warmed Jane's heart, receiving her message had warmed mine in return.

"I'd been questioning parts of my journey," I shared with Jane, "and had perhaps lost sight of the important things in some of the dimmer moments. I needed a reminder as to why I had packed up everything and headed out west in a Daisymobile."

Her message had certainly given me exactly that.

~

Daisy had passed away in 2006. I was curious so I just had to ask Jane what made Daisy such a loved and revered woman. She described Daisy's loving character, her huge heart and infectious sense of humour. Her description brought back memories of my dearly-loved grandmother who passed away many years ago. If she was anything like my Grandma, I could appreciate the kind of person that Daisy must have been.

I smiled when Jane mentioned that Daisy also enjoyed camping outings with her husband in a motor home that apparently looked much like mine. It seemed like the Daisy spirit was very much alive and well in Nanaimo that day, in more daisy ways than one.

But hey, that's the power of a daisy.

chapter 52

A Few Musings about 'Stuff'

A friend asked me whether I missed stuff.

"No."

I had gotten rid of much of my stuff before I'd left Ottawa. Most of my furniture and possessions I'd sold or given away, whittling my life down to a small storage unit and minimal belongings I'd brought on board *Miss Daisy*.

It had made my life very simple. Without an expansive space to fill, I simply focused on the essentials. I questioned every purchase. Did I really need it? Did I wish to store it or carry it around with me? I will never forget the lesson of my dead, but not-so dearly departed stability ball.

I don't know why having stuff is so valued. Yet many folks continue to want more stuff, bigger stuff or fancier stuff.

I never did have much stuff and I still don't have much stuff. Nor do I miss having stuff. It's quite freeing having less stuff.

It allows you to find out what matters the most.

What I discovered in my travels was this: it's what's inside you that counts. That's the most valuable asset you'll ever have.

The rest is just stuff.

chapter 53

Some Wishful Thinking About the Life Purpose Fairy

I sometimes wished that our human search for deeper spiritual meaning, true happiness and our life purpose couldn't be just a tad easier. After many months, make that years, of trying to find my way, I was longing for a visit from the 'Life Purpose Fairy'.

In the past couple of weeks I'd received many curious nudges and messages from all directions. I just wanted to wake up one day and find a note under my pillow with very clear instructions as to next steps. *Dear Heather, You won't believe this, but the Hokey Pokey really is what it's all about! So just do the Hokey Pokey more often! Your friend, the Life Purpose Fairy.* Well, perhaps more specific directions than that but you get the idea.

Sadly, the Life Purpose Fairy never came to visit and leave such a note. I was even willing to swing a three-way deal with the Tooth Fairy. I would have been happy to leave a tooth under my pillow in exchange for some insight into my ultimate destiny. *Save the small change for the kiddies Tooth Fairy, I just want to barter a molar for some life wisdom.* Isn't that what wisdom teeth are for?

That is not how the system works although I already knew that anyway. Some days I just wanted to take the shortcut if there was one.

Finding our way is kind of like playing Pin the Tail on the Donkey. We have a general idea about which direction to go in but some guidance from the audience is helpful.

The signs are always there for us if only we choose to see or hear them. I knew that I could always count on daisies to point me in the right direction.

They had lined the route that had brought me to Nanaimo and when I lost sight of them in the midst of winter, I wondered whether I'd been led astray. The events of the past few weeks quickly extinguished any thinking that I wasn't in the right place, doing the right thing or moving in the right direction.

~

It had all began with Jane's email and her story of her dearly-loved mother-in-law Daisy. Our synchronous encounter will forever remain one of the most unforgettable highlights of my adventure with *Miss Daisy*.

Then I met Gail. She'd approached me one day on her bicycle as I was fuelling up at the gas station.

"Are you Wild Daisy?" she asked.

"Yes." I replied. Gail mentioned that she owned a motor home too but hadn't travelled with it since her husband died two years earlier. She'd been too afraid to venture on her own. Her husband had always driven their rig, she'd always sat in the passenger seat.

Gail asked many questions as to how I'd managed my travels as a solo female. It seemed to be a big leap for her. "You could do it," I assured her, sensing that she really wanted to give it a try. She seemed relieved, as if it was exactly what she needed to hear.

"My mom would have loved your rig," Gail then said. "Her name was Daisy and I just love daisies." I simply smiled. Once again, life had brilliantly coordinated a surprise meeting of two souls who needed to meet each other.

As we bid each other goodbye, Gail's appearance seemed brighter. She thanked me for our chat. "I'm going to travel around the area on my own this summer, thanks for the inspiration Wild Daisy!" were her parting words.

Three weeks later I ran into Gail at the laundromat. With great excitement, she shared that she'd just come back from her first solo weekend away.

~

There were still moments when I debated a permanent move to Nanaimo. My brief interaction with a fellow dog-walker helped calm my concerns rather quickly one day.

I bumped into Joanne and her dog, Ginger one day while I was walking Daisy 'Mo. As dog-owners often do, we introduced our dogs first. Joanne told me that Ginger's favourite playmate was a dog named Daisy. I knew in my heart that I needed to pay attention to whatever Joanne had to say.

Joanne had moved to Nanaimo from Toronto 26 years ago. She knew what it meant to start over in a new place, leaving good friends and family behind.

I told Joanne that I was a new transplant to Nanaimo, in the midst of trying to sort out my next steps. I candidly shared that I missed my friends back home and was trying to reconcile my thoughts and feelings around that part of my life.

Joanne replied, "Heather, you seem to be a friendly, outgoing kind of person. You'll make new friends in no time. Meanwhile, you cannot lose your good friends back in Ottawa who are truly your friends."

True enough and likely what I needed to hear. Only when I turned to say goodbye to her, did I realize that I'd been standing in a patch of hundreds of tiny daisies the entire time.

I just needed the reassurance. I knew in my heart that I was meant to stay in Nanaimo, at least for the time being. The daisies were all pointing in that direction. And so was the heather.

~

When spring arrived in Nanaimo, hundreds of bright daisies popped up on every lawn around town. A more favourable sign that my heart had brought me to the right place I could not have asked for. Yet, in spite of being surrounded by daisies, I continued to struggle with some major life decisions.

I'm sure the folks at Magical Dream Place headquarters must have been scratching their heads at me. "We organized the biggest display of wild daisies the world has ever seen and she's still not getting the message! Do we have to hit her in the side of the head with a Nanaimo bar?"

Fortunately, they opted not to waste a perfectly good Nanaimo bar and sent me another sign instead. Just to reassure me that I was indeed on the right path.

With the name Heather, I have some Scottish blood running through my veins. On special occasions, I may even have some good Scotch running through them too. I also have a fond connection with Scottish heather, the hardy plant that covers the hillsides in Scotland. In fact, I always thought that it only grew in Scotland.

While out on my walks with Daisy 'Mo, I noticed lovely purple-hued flowers in many Nanaimo gardens. *Hmm, that looks like heather, but it can't be because heather only grows in Scotland.*

This same conversation replayed in my head for several days. At the same time, I was having a conversation with life, asking for some nudges in the next direction. It was a conversation with a woman at the dog park that finally caused the light bulb to come on.

She: "It's a gorgeous day, perfect for working in my garden."

Me: "Yes, indeed."

She:" I have so much to do. I have to trim my heather today."

Me: (ears perking to attention) "Oh, you have heather in your garden?"

She: "Yes, loads of it."

Me: "Um, so, that's what I've been seeing around Nanaimo in people's gardens? That's heather?"

She: 'Yes, it's everywhere."

Heather, the person, had been wandering and wondering around, looking for some clarity. Heather, the flowery plant had been staring back at her the entire time.

"The answer is in the heather," the flowers seemed to say to me. "You're on the right path."

I was excited to learn that heather flourished not only in Scotland.

Heather seemed to thrive with her roots firmly planted in Nanaimo too.

~

For some reason I still had a hunch that I'd be travelling back to Ottawa though. I just wasn't sure when or how. I sensed that something was brewing on the horizon. At the beginning of July, I had to travel to Calgary for a few weeks and wondered about heading east from there.

Thankfully, I was feeling more positive about life at this point. My financial picture hadn't changed but somehow I felt more relaxed about it. I simply had more faith that I was on the right path, doing the right thing, whatever that was on any given day.

As I sat in Starbucks later that day, the Dixie Chicks sang in the background. "...it takes the shape of a place out west but what it holds for her she hasn't guessed yet...." I'd never paid close attention to those lyrics before but suddenly they held my attention and made perfect sense.

Maybe the Life Purpose Fairy hadn't left me a note but at least I got some insight from the Chicks. They were likely right. It would take the shape of a place out west but what it would hold for me, I hadn't guessed yet.

chapter 54

The Shift Hit the Fan

Like friends, RVs come into your life for a reason, a season or a lifetime. I had always known that one day I would goodbye to *Miss Daisy*, just as I had said goodbye to my house. I felt that day was getting closer.

There had been many layers to peel off this onion of a life journey and transition I had embarked upon. The latest awakening included the awareness and acceptance that my destiny had brought me to Nanaimo for good reason and likely for a more permanent stay.

I felt stuck at this crossroads however. *Do I continue to travel? Do I stay in Nanaimo? If I do, where do I live? Do I head back to Ottawa? How do I pay for it all?* A decision of some sort needed to be made.

Thus I decided that it was time to take an action step and see how things unfolded from there. A few hours later, I put *Miss Daisy* up for sale.

There comes a time to move on and a time to let go in order to welcome what comes next. Maybe I would discover what came next by letting go of *Miss Daisy*. Not only that but selling *Miss Daisy* would also release me from the financial and logistical burden of caring for her in her old age and inject some much-needed cash into my bank account.

Without question, *Miss Daisy* had served me well. The thought of parting ways with my faithful travelling companion left me with some feelings of trepidation, I'll admit. I'd experienced those same feelings when I initially put my house up for sale.

The time had come for the next part of the journey, for another leap forward. *Miss Daisy* had become some sort of comfort zone for me and once again, it was time to step onto *terra familiara*.

Notwithstanding that the space kept getting smaller and smaller as Daisy 'Mo got bigger and bigger. She could easily jump up on the kitchen table, which she treated as her own all-you-can-eat buffet. I worried that one day she might steal the keys to *Miss Daisy* and take her on a wild joyride around town.

The announcement that I'd begun searching for the next Daisymobile driver caused a small riot amongst my friends. "What? You can't sell *Miss Daisy*! Where will you live? What will you do?" and "Are you leaving town?"

Surprisingly, these comments weren't even from my mother.

I honestly didn't know the answers to those questions. I just needed to take one step without worrying what the next one was going to be. By putting *Miss Daisy* up for sale, I was merely saying to the universe,

Hey, I'm ready for something else. I'm open to whatever possibilities you send my way.

When I'd put my house up for sale, I didn't know what the eventual outcome would like look either. I certainly hadn't anticipated that it would look like a giant daisy-covered RV. This time around, I was hopeful that things would also work out much better than I ever could imagine. Like maybe I'd end up living in a daisy-shaped house and driving a daisy-covered spaceship? Or something fun like that.

So *Miss Daisy* was for sale and I still had no idea as to where I might live next. I only hoped that some sort of shift was about to hit the fan.

to use and a hot tub was like being booked in the Presidential Suite at the Hilton as far as I was concerned.

It felt like an oasis after a long journey across the desert.

I was tired and in much need of a rest. I was tired of facing challenge upon challenge. I was tired of not eating properly. I was tired of living day-to-day financially. I was tired of staring into a void of uncertainty. I was tired of trying to figure things out. I was tired of sleeping in a parking lot or on a downtown street. I was tired of living in an RV. I was just plain tired.

Yeah, I know. *This is how it's meant to be.*

I just needed a break from it all. This idyllic mini-vacation was exactly what the life doctor had ordered.

Daisy 'Mo and I woke up each morning and enjoyed a hike on the nearby trails. Lush ferns, barred owls and slugs the size of my feet were some of the interesting things we'd see. Actually the slugs were kind of icky at first, but I tried to appreciate their role in the forest ecosystem. After all, you shouldn't judge a slug by its lack of cover. Sometimes Daisy 'Mo and I would simply sit in *Miss Daisy* and watch the deer walk by on the lawn. Rather, I would sit and watch the deer. Daisy 'Mo would yelp with excitement at the top of her doggie lungs, "Let me out of here so I can go chase them!"

On other days, I would have to clear rabbit carcasses off the lawn.

I awoke one morning to the grotesque sight of animal remains outside. I bolt at top speed at the first sight of a mouse so I was not at all excited about having to confront a dead bunny. Some things are a fact of rural life, I realize that, but when it comes to hawks dropping dead things from the sky, I suffer from N.I.M.B.Y. syndrome, as in 'not in my backyard'!

I couldn't leave the bunny carcass there. It was a hot June day for one thing. Secondly, Detective Daisy 'Mo, Terrier Private Eye, would definitely want to investigate the scene of the crime.

I slowly approached the grisly scene with the longest shovel I could find. En route, I debated whether I could approach a neighbour for help.

(Knock, knock.) "Hi, I'm Heather, I'm house-sitting across the street. I don't need to borrow a cup of sugar, but would you like to help me get rid of some dead rabbit carcasses instead?" I suspected that might not be the best way to introduce myself to the neighbourhood.

I closed my eyes and inched closer. I'm the girl who fainted when I got my ears pierced. My queasiness was being put to the test with this gruesome wildlife murder.

What happened next would have made a wonderful scene in the movie *Blair Witch Project*. It involved a few piercing screams (mine), a dropped head, a frantic run in the woods and eventual burial of the evidence.

On the other hand, most of my house-sitting days were lovely. It was heavenly to be able to enjoy long showers any time of day, every day. I could do my laundry as needed. I lingered in the outdoor hot tub each night, watching the moon and the stars.

There was only the one day that was a tad on the macabre side.

It was an experience in contrast during my travels. Death versus life. Green space versus a parking lot. Stationary versus mobile. Plugged in versus unplugged. Luxury versus the basics. You can't appreciate one without also experiencing the other.

So I guess that's how it's meant to be.

map. Alex then took over the town, for the princely sum of $135, and became mayor, police chief, fireman, Tim Horton's drive-thru attendant, whatever it took to keep the town going.

Over time, he eventually paid off the back taxes until Holley was able to reclaim its town status and earn the right to appear on the map again. How often do you get a chance to meet someone who'd actually put a place on the map?

When Alex had retired, he knew that he absolutely had to do something to stimulate himself and his life. He didn't want to end up as many others do, beginning a slow, unpleasant decline into old age.

Instead, he thought he'd drift at sea. He bought himself a large sailboat, even though he was a landlubber Albertan who'd never sailed. At the age of 70, he learned to sail, not without a few mishaps mind you.

He told me a story about one of his first outings on his new boat. While attempting to leave Nanaimo harbour one morning his boat kept spinning uncontrollably and he couldn't figure out why. Evidently, he came dangerously close to taking out several nearby boats and marina buildings, which would have caused thousands of dollars in damages. Suddenly my little crushed air-conditioner under the bridge incident looked very novice by comparison.

It's quite curious how our brains work or perhaps more accurately, *don't* work, under such circumstances. Just as I'd thought I could stuff a large RV under a small bridge, Alex thought that perhaps he was simply turning the wheel the wrong way. It was only after an hour or so of going in circles in the harbour that he discovered that the steering unit was completely non-functional.

Alex certainly didn't live life in a straight line nor did he sail in one. In his mid-70s, he spends winters in Calgary and summers in Nanaimo, living in his small camper van and spending most days on the water in his boat. As someone living the unconventional retirement of his dreams, I found him an inspiration. I'd certainly be happy to follow in his wake in my 70s!

And then there's Helen, without question a woman who leaves no doubt as to what's possible at any age. I met Helen one day while walking Daisy 'Mo in one of the local dog parks. She walked with a cane and I admired her gumption for coming to an off-leash dog park where dogs run in all directions and can easily knock you off your feet. While Daisy 'Mo frolicked with Helen's two corgis, we chatted.

"That's some wild RV in the parking lot, isn't it?" she said, glancing in the direction of *Miss Daisy*.

"It's mine," I replied.

Helen laughed and shared that she also owned an RV. She spoke of her love of travelling with her two dogs and mentioned that she'd just returned from a one-week trip to the interior of British Columbia.

Her RVing lifestyle wouldn't have been all that unusual except for the fact that Helen was 93. She travelled frequently throughout the summer, driving her 25-foot rig all by herself.

Some might say that a 93-year old shouldn't be driving a car let alone an RV. Helen, on the other hand, might argue that some 39-year olds shouldn't be driving a car either and instead experience what life looks like from behind the wheel of an RV.

Thank goodness for people like Helen and Alex who bust through the norms of stereotypes that the world places upon us and our dreams. Thank goodness for people like Helen and Alex who show us that our dreams may be, and perhaps need to be, unconventional. Thank goodness for people like Helen and Alex who show us what is truly possible, at any age.

We're never too old. We're never too 'anything' to live our dreams.

chapter 58

Happy Cannabis Day

Every year on July 1, Canadians celebrate Canada's birthday coast to coast. It's a national holiday known as Canada Day. Or in some parts of Canada, it's also known as Cannabis Day. For the first time in my life, I celebrated both.

For the past 10 years, I'd celebrated Canada Day in the nation's capital, Ottawa. The traditional festivities such as partying on Parliament Hill, perhaps a trip to the beach, a BBQ, always followed by the evening fireworks show generally made up the agenda of the day. I had always conformed, Canadian style, and felt that this year called for something different.

On Canada/Cannabis Day, I headed to Vancouver to meet up with my friend Margo who was visiting from Ottawa. Margo would be riding shotgun in *Miss Daisy* for the upcoming week, after which I'd be heading to Calgary for three weeks. Margo and I had decided to go to Sarah McLachlan's Lilith Fair concert and spend a few hours walking around downtown Vancouver beforehand.

It was during our pre-concert meanderings that we came upon an alternative way to celebrate July 1. We enthusiastically approached a downtown park that seemed to have some good Canada Day fun going on. Red and white flags waved in the air, vendors were selling things from their tents and happy people were milling about. We wandered inside to investigate the fun.

"Wait a second, something's wrong with that flag?" I said to Margo. The official red maple leaf that normally adorns the middle of the Canadian flag had been replaced by some other kind of plant.

"That looks like...." Before Margo could finish her sentence I saw the sign.

"Happy Cannabis Day!" *Toto, I've got a feeling we're not in Kansas anymore.*

I am not sure of the origins of Cannabis Day however it certainly seemed to have its own loyal following. It was my first cannabis event of any kind (honest Mom!), and Margo and I wandered around like kids in a very alternative kind of candy shop. Vendors offered us substances that we'd never even heard of. When I asked one of them whether the event was legal, the reply was, "Yeah, well, sort of..." Whatever that, um, yeah, sort of meant I wasn't well, sort of, entirely sure.

If not for the unusual scents wafting through the air, the scene could have easily been mistaken for a neighbourhood bake sale. A delicious-looking array of brownies, cookies and squares taunted us at every turn. I don't like to say no in life, especially to baked goods of any kind. In the spirit of adventure, Margo and I looked at each other, "Hmmm, should we?"

It seemed like the West Coast thing to do. It was actually something that I'd had on my 'West Coast bucket list' since arriving. Climb a mountain. Swim in the ocean. Try some dope. "What the heck?" we said and bought ourselves a package of 'special' homemade cookies.

Alternative baked goods in hand, we headed off to the concert, giddy as school kids who were trying to sneak something by on their teacher. As cannabis novices, we were filled with many questions. "When should we eat these? We have to time them so we can get home on the bus! We should eat them well before Sarah comes on stage…. I wonder if they sell special milk to go with these cookies?"

We ended up serving our cookies with a side of Sheryl Crow. It must have been divine dope timing as Sheryl wished the crowd "Happy Cannabis Day!" the moment she took to the stage. Even Sheryl was caught up in the Cannabis Day celebrations! *All I want to do is to have some fun and you know what Sheryl, I've got a feeling I'm not the only one.*

Margo and I bit into our cookies. They might have a following amongst the cannabis-loving crowd, but they never would have taken a ribbon at the county fair, that's for sure. I know, I know, should I be such a food critic about a dope-infused biscuit?

It's just that I like my baked goods. I like my cookies to be chewy, sweet and delicious. These were rather crunchy, dry and ho-hum. It was a good thing that they did have the cannabis in them because I certainly wasn't going to get high on the culinary experience alone.

Nonetheless, we ate them and waited for the cannabis to put the 'happy' into our Happy Cannabis Day. As we waited several free-spirited dancers gathered on the lawn nearby, entertaining us with their mesmerizing hula-hoop skills. Judging by the level of their enthusiasm and frantic body gyrations, I suspected they'd had a few baked goods or something of their own too.

Thankfully, the side effects of our cookies did not seem to include the overwhelming urge to join this wild band of dancing outlaws or to run around in our underpants, as we witnessed one 'enthusiastic' concert-dweller doing. We kept our clothes on, giggled a lot and enjoyed a new cannabis twist on our Canada Day celebrations.

Sarah McLachlan came onstage to end the concert. Her sultry voice filled the air as I gazed around at the mountains, the ocean and the open sky above. The side effects of that moment were far more potent than those of the cookies. For that, I could only feel immensely grateful.

I felt grateful for the experience that had dramatically changed my life. I felt grateful for the country I had travelled across with my heart.

And I felt incredibly grateful that the next cookie I'd pick up would be chewy, sweet and delicious.

chapter 59

Miss Daisy Loses Steam

Life comes with highs, sometimes from the side effects of cookies, and life comes with lows. I guess you could say that I'd just come off a high so I shouldn't have been all that surprised when life decided to send me a low. Still, I am only human so I can be forgiven for being less than thrilled with my plummet from sky high.

Life had been going splendidly in the post-Lilith Fair days. My friend Margo and I were enjoying seeing the sights around Nanaimo and had just finished spending the day on Denman Island watching a family of nesting eagles. We were headed to Tofino, on the west coast of Vancouver Island, where we planned to spend a couple of days relaxing and enjoying the beaches. *Miss Daisy*, however, had other plans in mind.

Thirty minutes into the drive, I began to notice that *Miss Daisy* wasn't driving with her usual vim and vigour. She began to sputter and I began to break into a sweat of nervousness. At least Captain Kirk had Scotty to help him through those emergency situations when the Starship *Enterprise* lost power. There was no little Scotsman in the back of *Miss Daisy* shouting in his thick accent, "We're losing power, Captain Heather, but don't worry. I'm firing up the backup system, we should be good in a few minutes."

Instead, *Miss Daisy* lost all power and I pulled off to the side of the road. A small explosion erupted under the hood, followed by a huge blast of steam that billowed from her underbelly. A smelly cloud of smoke and steam filled the cabin as Margo and I evacuated. We would not be going to Tofino.

I know that all things happen for a reason but I was a tad upset with the universe that day.

Why does this have to happen while my friend was visiting? Why now, when we were headed to gorgeous Tofino? Why now, when I didn't need another costly RV repair? Why now, when I had to leave for Calgary in only a few days time? And why another challenge when I'd already jumped through so many hurdles? What's the reason for this?

After calling for a tow truck, I walked along the side of the road asking those very questions.

Dear God, why?

I stopped in my footsteps and glanced into the ditch. Standing there, all by itself, was a single wild daisy. There wasn't another wild daisy anywhere in sight. I smiled, thankful for the reassuring sign that there was some sort of divine reason for the calamitous radiator explosion.

It seemed that the heavens had also conspired to take care of me by sending me Ron, the tow truck guy. They must have known that I would not have made it through the experience without an injection of humour.

Somewhere along the drive back to Nanaimo, I mentioned to Ron that I was a writer and aspiring author.

"Well, if you want an interesting book, ride with a few tow truck drivers and you'll get some interesting stories!" After spending 45 minutes on the road with Ron, I would have to agree, particularly if I was interested in sharing gruesome tales of vehicle accidents and dismembered bodies. I will always value Ron's advice to buy a vehicle that offers a good steel buffer in case of an accident, not one of those cars that "are just chicken wire wrapped in plastic." I trusted his judgement and experience on that.

A book about the tow trucking lifestyle might have some appeal I suppose. How many people really know about the secret life of a tow truck driver? As Ron candidly shared, part of his job is to leave people feeling happy after their tow, an admirable and lofty goal considering the circumstances that often lead to one's vehicle being towed. Being towed by Ron had certainly given me a lift in more ways than one.

I couldn't avoid laughing as he shared what life can be like for someone who is constantly on call.

"You can be in the middle of smooching with a woman when your pager goes off and it's like – can you just hold that babe, I'll be back in about four hours, and I'll be all greasy and stuff." That kind of challenge might explain why Ron had gone through three wives. Either that or it may have been his toothless grin and shortage of hair, I wasn't sure which.

The humour was welcome as Margo and I were looking at spending a glamorous evening camped at the back of the truck service centre in the industrial part of Nanaimo. Suffice to say that I don't think that was the kind of holiday spot that Margo had in mind for her vacation, much as I tried to sell the charm of the experience. Not everyone was as excited about a level parking spot as I was at that point in my RV life.

A full diagnosis of *Miss Daisy's* 'hot flash' as I called it would have to wait until the next morning when a mechanic was available. Ron had assured me, "Don't worry, it'll be a cinch popping that radiator out and you'll be back on the road in no time...."

With those words, Ron's job was complete. He'd left me feeling happy, humoured and optimistic after the tow.

~

Unfortunately, I wasn't as happy Monday morning after it took Mike the mechanic nearly seven hours to wiggle the radiator out of the tight confines of *Miss Daisy's* engine. I could have used either Ron's sense of humour or another Cannabis Day cookie to help get me through that day. My spirits were lower than a snake's belly.

hood. She'd overheated again, leaving me stranded in the 35 degree Celsius heat of the Fraser Canyon, with a six-month-old puppy and no cellular phone service. Where the hell was tough guy Rambo to come and rescue me when I needed him?

Umm, hello, can I speak to someone at Life Headquarters? This is NOT the kind of adventure I was looking for!

Here's a piece of good advice for you when travelling through remote areas. Always have a bicycle handy. I would have had a long walk if not for *Miss Daisy Too* who wheeled me to the nearest general store a few kilometres away to use the payphone. First, I made a frantic, teary-eyed phone call to my family. My poor mother had to relive her worst nightmare. I was as close to becoming a trucker as I'd ever come and now I was swearing like one as I recounted the day's events.

Next I called the Canadian Automobile Association for another tow, this time from Chad. I was probably Chad's worse nightmare too. I cried during the entire ride back into town. I was only a few disasters short of becoming a bad country song. "One minute I was living life on the road, the next I was being towed, it was a sad day when my RV died, oh Lord, how I cried and cried...."

At 5 p.m. that Friday afternoon, Chad dropped *Miss Daisy* and I off at the rear parking lot of Gardner GMC. Surrounded by gorgeous mountains and a sea of shiny, new vehicles, this would be my new home for an indeterminate amount of time.

~

I couldn't complain about the hospitality at Gardner GMC. They welcomed *Miss Daisy* and I as if we were family. Well, with her Chevy 454 engine she certainly was. They kindly let me plug my rig into their building, which meant that I had a functioning fridge and air conditioning, which I dearly needed in the heat. *Thank goodness I had crushed my old air conditioning unit back in Winnipeg.* Air conditioning karma had served me well as I'm certain my old unit wouldn't have keep me nearly as cool in the wake of *Miss Daisy*'s hot flash.

A mechanic wouldn't be able to look at *Miss Daisy* until the following morning so the helpful folks at Gardner suggested a few local sights to see to help pass the evening.

I wasn't much in the mood for sightseeing though. Instead, I took a walk to a nearby park and sat on a bench, gazing upon the waters of the Fraser River. And I cried. Frustrated, tired and angry tears. *Dear Lord, why is this happening?* The situation just didn't make any sense to me.

Even the patch of wild daisies that I noticed growing a few feet from the bench didn't make sense to me either.

~

I was a bit of a mess. I had staked everything I had on this journey of the heart and the pursuit of my dreams. I had fully invested my emotional and spiritual self. I'd left family and friends. I'd dwindled my life savings and I'd shared my journey publicly on my blog. I'd also just spent over $3,000 repairing *Miss Daisy* for what turned out to be a 150 km trip.

I did not welcome nor understand this additional calamity or expense.

Amidst my tears, many questions ran through my mind. *What's wrong with Miss Daisy? My bank account is already nearly empty. I can't afford another repair! How long will I be in Hope? What kind of ironic joke is the universe playing on me to land me in a place called Hope?*

I didn't have any answers. The only thing I could do was to try to get some sleep.

The next morning I did get the answer to one of my questions. Sadly, it wasn't the answer I wanted.

~

Saturday looked very bright when it began. Warm sunshine greeted the day, which filled me with rays of optimism.

My surroundings were idyllic. Hope is a vibrant town that lies in a picturesque mountain setting at the east end of the sprawling Fraser Valley. Forested mountains surround town and the mighty Fraser River flows past its doorstep. Right outside *Miss Daisy's* door the town's namesake mountain, Mount Hope, stood strong and tall.

Thankfully life had blessed me with exterior beauty, which helped soften the internal blow of bad news about *Miss Daisy*.

It didn't take long for John the mechanic to offer up his diagnosis. Several times he tried to resuscitate *Miss Daisy's* engine but to no avail. She was gone.

"She's got a blown head gasket," he said, and then continued to explain in mechanical jargon speak what had happened to her radiator and engine. The only words that my daisy-brain understood were, "she needs a new engine."

It sounded like a diagnosis that was far beyond my budgetary means. I would have to wait until Monday morning to get an exact price of a new engine or an engine rebuild.

I may have landed in Hope but things weren't looking very hopeful.

~

There are times in life when you just need to commiserate with a friend. I felt more than qualified to indulge myself in one of those times.

I called my friend Trish in Vancouver with whom I shared my latest woes and my latest whoas. The demise of *Miss Daisy's* engine had issued a big 'whoa' to my life and travel plans, which was directly related to my current state of woe.

I sobbed into the phone as Trish listened patiently.

"What the hell am I going to do? My bank account is empty and now I'm stranded in the parking lot of a car dealership! I don't have another place to go to and all my belongings are on board *Miss Daisy*. AND I have a puppy with me. This is not how I'd expected things to unfold."

When I finished my rant, Trish simply said, "Whoa."

Yes, exactly.

Trish offered to drive up from Vancouver that day and visit., "Yes, please come!" I enthusiastically replied.

We found the perfect place at a tranquil lake near town where I tried to sooth my spirit in its pristine waters. It was also the ideal spot for Trish to give me a gentle kick in the posterior and prompt me to find the opportunity in the situation. I had commiserated, now I needed to be nudged in a different direction.

"Heather, you could feel sorry for yourself and hopeless about everything or you could feel powerful about the opportunity that this situation presents . . . which would you prefer?" Trish asked.

I laughed.

"Gee Trish, when you put it that way...."

It was a brilliant question and one that quickly jarred me out of my misery and into looking at the situation with a fresh perspective.

I did have to ask why life would present me with this scenario. Maybe it wasn't really about *Miss Daisy*'s failed engine. Maybe it was really about me. Maybe I needed to find the power and the opportunity in the midst of everything life had thrown at me. And maybe I also needed to learn about hope.

"Life doesn't give you what you want, it gives you what you need", as my wise friend Tara always says.

While I couldn't yet see the light at the end of the tunnel I knew that life always works out somehow. I didn't know what I was going to do about *Miss Daisy*. I didn't know where I would be in one week's time. I didn't know where I was going to get my next shower. I didn't know how I was going to pay for anything. I didn't know how or where I'd be headed once I did leave Hope. *Miss Daisy* had been my vehicle and my residence for the past year.

After the tears had subsided, my heart told me not to worry. How could I? I was surrounded by Hope. Life does have an ironic sense of humour I must say.

Which would also explain the banner that I noticed while I was walking down Main Street that day:

"Experience Hope – One Day is Not Enough."

No, it's certainly not.

chapter 61

A Few Lessons in Hope

I'd never given hope much thought before. As I was literally surrounded by Hope, now I didn't have much choice.

I performed some quick research on the meaning of hope and came up with this simple definition of my own.

Hope is a belief in a positive outcome related to events and circumstance in one's life. Hope is a feeling that something desired may happen when the outlook may or may not warrant it.

I certainly needed a dose of hope. I needed to believe that something positive would come out of what felt like very dim circumstances. Whether I wanted it or not, I'd be getting a dose of Hope as well.

If I was going to learn about hope, it seems that life had coincidentally arranged the perfect classroom.

~

Dick Gardner, one of the owners of Gardner GMC, delivered the bad news with the sensitivity of a surgeon informing a family member that they'd lost a loved one on the operating table. He must have sensed how I felt.

With an empathic look on his face, Dick informed me that it would cost at least $10,000 to revive *Miss Daisy's* engine. As that was a few zeros more than I had in my bank account at the time, I told Dick to put a 'Do Not Resuscitate' order on *Miss Daisy's* file. She had arrived at her final resting place in Hope.

I had no idea what I was going to do next. When you don't know what to do, you need to do something. So I did something. I went for a hike up to the top of Mount Hope and looked at Hope from a different point of view.

~

I'd always believed that there would be a positive outcome from my journey of the heart. But it's easy to have a positive outlook and feel hopeful when life's going well.

While crossing Canada on my daisy adventure, it was easy to believe in my big dreams. It was certainly more challenging as I sat broke and stranded in my conked out Daisymobile in the middle of British Columbia, wondering where I would end up next.

As I gazed at my situation, I didn't see a proverbial pot of gold at the end of a joyful rainbow. But when I gazed down from the lookout at the top of Mount Hope, I saw a breathtaking panorama of beauty. The little town of Hope appeared microscopically small from my vantage point, dwarfed by the magnitude of magnificent surrounding mountains. Not a cloud in the blue sky. The brilliant sunshine warmed my spirit as I revelled in the view.

It was a view I would not have enjoyed had I not been forced to stop in Hope. Maybe I needed the change in perspective, the opportunity to experience the beauty in my circumstances. Or perhaps *regardless* of my circumstances.

As I sat atop Mount Hope, my worries and questions seemed to fade. Curiously, they seemed to be replaced with something else. I think it was hope.

~

What was I going to do with *Miss Daisy*? That was a good question.

Conveniently, my automobile association membership had covered the costs of my previous two tows. My membership had expired in timely fashion the day after my arrival in Hope, which meant that any future towing would come at a premium price. The thought of paying for *Miss Daisy* to be towed off the lot to a scrap yard would have only added financial injury and mental insult to my already precarious situation.

There was no way I would send my precious girl to a scrap yard either. She still had some things to offer life, such as her working fridge and air conditioning unit, not to mention her grooving daisy attire.

Leave it to life to orchestrate the perfect solution in these kinds of circumstances.

I'd just been wondering how I could repay the folks at the dealership for allowing me to camp in the back of their lot for several days. Notwithstanding the obvious promotional opportunity that having *Miss Daisy* parked in their lot was offering. "Follow your heart wherever it takes you" makes for a nice suggestive marketing message when it comes to car buying too.

Not everyone sees it that way however so I still had to find a home for *Miss Daisy*. Rather coincidentally one morning, Dick Gardner mentioned that one of his mechanics was interested in her.

Evidently, Bill was going through a rough patch in life and needed a cheap place to live. He was facing a divorce and some other life challenges and didn't have much money either.

As I chatted with a rather shy Bill in the garage that day, I asked him what he thought of the daisies on *Miss Daisy*.

"They're cool. I mean, I wouldn't have put 'em on myself, you know. As a guy and all…."

Regardless, it was a match made in daisy heaven. I'd found *Miss Daisy*'s new owner. And Bill had found his new, albeit slightly effeminate home.

Agreeing on a price was easy. All I asked of Bill was that he tow *Miss Daisy* away, once I was ready to leave Hope. In a matter of minutes, we had ourselves a mutually agreeable deal.

I surely could have used the money if I'd tried to sell her, but giving *Miss Daisy* to Bill just felt like the right thing to do. The thought of *Miss Daisy* spending her remaining days in a town called Hope appealed to me. I also liked the idea of giving a bit of hope to the life of someone who seemed to need it as much as I did.

It was certainly a positive outcome to the events surrounding *Miss Daisy's* demise.

Now I only needed to find a home for myself and my pup, Daisy 'Mo. I had hope that that search would come together just as easily.

chapter 62

The Proverbial Fork
in the Road

After five days in their parking lot, the guys at Gardner GMC had begun to joke about installing flowers and planter boxes around *Miss Daisy*. Meanwhile, I joked about becoming a resident car salesman. *Buy any new vehicle and I'll throw in a Daisymobile for free!*

I'd adjusted nicely to life in their midst. The tap outside their building offered a local source of water and I referred to the salesroom bathroom as my 'ensuite'. I was able to enjoy conversations around the water cooler with the employees without ever having to do any actual work. A hot shower was available at the local recreation facility and Dairy Queen was just down the street. Only five minutes away was the trailhead for the hike that led to Mount Hope Lookout, where Daisy 'Mo and I ventured daily. It may not have been a five-star resort, but it offered its own amenities.

I was also within walking distance of the charming Main Street, which was lined with quaint shops. Wonderful artisan wood carvings were displayed throughout town including a large gorilla-looking animal that I thought resembled an escapee from the *Planet of the Apes*. A friend kindly corrected me when she saw the photo I'd taken, "Um Heather, that's a Sasquatch." Right. I'm in the mountains,

I'm not having an interplanetary experience.

A beautiful tree-lined park sits in the middle of town. Daisy 'Mo and I enjoyed spending time relaxing and gazing at the mountains, playing ball or listening to the weekly jazz concerts that took place in the band shell.

Of all the places I could have been stranded, Hope was indeed a beautiful spot. Not only that, it was welcoming, warm and friendly too. I even had the opportunity to go a date if I'd wanted to!

One afternoon, I was passing by the Haz Moh Restaurant, home of fine Canadian-Chinese cuisine, while out on a walk with Daisy 'Mo. Out of the restaurant walked a fellow carrying a foam takeout container loaded up with a colourful array of food. "Looks good!" I commented as I walked by. Let me clarify that my eyes were on his food, not on him.

"Take your dog home honey and come on back. I'll buy ya dinner," he graciously offered. Sadly, an invite for takeout Canadian-Chinese cuisine was the best proposition I'd had in weeks.

Not that I could have embarked upon any sort of long-term relationship anyways. I knew that I would soon be leaving Hope. To where, well, that's what I didn't yet know.

~

I had always planned and expected my adventure with *Miss Daisy* to end differently, somehow returning to Ottawa where it had all began. Or maybe that's what I'd *hoped* would happen. My shock that life had unceremoniously orchestrated other plans had not yet dissipated. However, between dealing with my own disappointment at the turn of events or dealing with the disappointment of others, I don't know which was more difficult to manage.

Yes, I felt disappointed. Life had dealt me a hand of cards that was radically different than what I'd expected and I didn't know how to play it. To make matters worse, my ordeal was on public display. Hundreds of friends and acquaintances had followed my travels via my blog and regular posts on Facebook. Sometimes their comments were harder to take than the pain of my own thoughts. People mourned the loss of *Miss Daisy*, openly sharing their sadness that my journey was 'over'. They expressed their disappointment that they wouldn't be able to read about the tales of *Miss Daisy* anymore. Some simply suggested that I should buy another RV to replace *Miss Daisy*, having no idea how empty my bank account was at the time. Without the ability to walk in my shoes or sit in my RV, many observers were more than willing to offer up armchair advice as to what they thought I should do.

At times I felt that I had failed. I had failed to complete my journey as I'd planned, as I'd said that I would. I had failed to live up to my own expectations. I had failed to fulfil the expectations that others had thrust upon me.

Or had I? Was this situation just as much a part of my journey of the heart as all of the other joyful times?

My circumstances were what they were, but the interpretation of the events surrounding them varied considerably. Bombarded with opinions and advice, I was feeling pulled in all directions and finding it difficult if not impossible to hear what my own heart was saying anymore.

The curtain was drawn on the well-meaning circus of bystanders the day one friend brazenly called me and said, "Do you want to hear what I think you should do?" *No actually. No, I really don't.*

For the next three days I turned off my phone, vanished from cyberspace and stopped listening to the commentary from the sidelines.

In those three days, I realized this. The only person who needed to make sense of my situation was me.

~

I'd always known that our relationship wouldn't be forever. Even so, I was sad to think of saying goodbye to my faithful travelling companion, *Miss Daisy*.

Miss Daisy had served me well. She'd taken me to places I'd always wanted to go and helped me meet people I wouldn't have met otherwise. She touched the hearts of many and caused smiles wherever she went. She'd given me the greatest adventure of my lifetime.

She'd also been my constant friend and companion. She was a source of comfort and was always there for me, rain or shine. She was also my biggest fan, always nudging me on my journey of the heart and encouraging me towards my dreams. She even helped point out daisies along the way.

It was an ending and a beginning for both of us. We'd both grown from our shared experience (well, *Miss Daisy* hadn't actually grown, but she did have a new A/C on her roof so she had done her share of self-improvement) and we were ready for the next stage of our lives.

Miss Daisy had given me strength, faith and wisdom. She'd taught me about dreams and possibilities. She'd shown me what freedom and happiness look like. She'd trained me to be resourceful. She'd helped me discover the real Me.

And now she was teaching me about hope.

It had never been my dream to live in or travel with *Miss Daisy* forever. I'd only wanted to follow my heart and have an adventure. She'd certainly granted me that.

Truly, could I have asked for anything more from one daisy-decalled RV?

~

I was entering the second week of my stay at the Château Gardner. As I hadn't succeeded in selling a single car, my future as a car salesman wasn't looking promising. It was time to figure out where and how I would be heading next.

I no longer had an address in Ottawa. I didn't have one in Nanaimo either. I didn't have an address anywhere anymore. The net result of these facts left me facing a conundrum.

So which direction do I head in now? East to Ottawa or West back to Nanaimo?

I wanted to take the path of least resistance. I'd had my share of overcoming obstacles, I wanted to go where the flow of life was easiest. I felt this was the right next direction.

Life seemed to flow in the direction of Nanaimo. I'd been able to quickly line up temporary accommodation there with a friend. Also rather coincidentally helpful was the fact that my brother, Ray, was in Vancouver on business and had agreed to come to Hope that weekend to help me pack and ship my things. It seemed like I'd be back to enjoying my Nanaimo bar lifestyle very soon.

There was one small glitch in the plan however. My accommodation in Nanaimo was not fully confirmed. A few emails had been exchanged between myself and my friend but I was still awaiting his call to confirm that all was a 'go.'

Ray and I spent our Saturday optimistically preparing to ship my things back to Nanaimo. I needed to head in one direction or another on Monday. On Saturday evening, when I still hadn't heard from my friend, it was time to implement Plan B. I called a friend in Ottawa and lined up a place to stay there, just in case.

When I went to bed that evening, I still didn't know which direction life would take me. It was like waiting for a presentation at the Academy Awards. The nominees had been announced, but the show had suddenly gone to a long commercial break. The winning city wouldn't be announced until after the commercials had finished, whenever that would be.

"And the winner is...."

The announcement came on Sunday morning when I still hadn't heard from my friend in Nanaimo. Life did not seem to be favouring my return there and it was decision time. At the proverbial eleventh hour, or 9 a.m. Sunday morning as was the case, the winning city was announced. I turned to my brother with mixed emotions and uttered, "I'm heading back to Ottawa. "

Within the hour, a flight for myself and Daisy 'Mo was booked, my belongings were on a Greyhound bus and I had a fixed address in Ottawa, at least a temporary one.

It was simply the path of least resistance.

~

That Sunday evening had a reflective air of melancholy as I prepared to move in a different direction and part ways with *Miss Daisy*. On one hand, I felt a sense of relief. On the other, I felt a sense of trepidation for what would come next.

A few things I knew for sure.

I had done something I once thought unimaginable. I had set myself free from the shackles of a lifeless existence and set sail in the direction of my deepest desires. I had fulfilled my dream to go across Canada and I'd had a blast doing it. I had learned to venture by myself. I had simplified my life and learned what truly matters most. I had discovered the real Me. And, I had taken some big steps in the direction of living the kind of life I'd always wanted.

Most importantly, I had learned to live life from the heart.

Things hadn't turned out the way that I'd expected. When you follow your heart you never really know what to expect. That, I believe, is the whole point.

I'd never wanted to reach my deathbed, glance back at my life and say, "I wish I had lived the life I'd wanted to. I wish I'd been comfortable enough to be Me. I wish I'd listened to my heart." I wanted my life to be an adventurous roller coaster ride, with its ups and downs, its thrills and turns, its scares and its laughter. I wanted to get off at the end and say, "Wow, *that* was a fun ride!"

It was simply time for the next part of the journey, another loop on the roller coaster, wherever that would take me.

I hoped that it would be somewhere positive and fun. Really, I hoped.

chapter 63

Meanwhile, Back in Ottawa

I was happy to finally arrive somewhere that wasn't a parking lot. After what felt like a whirlwind couple of weeks, I stood on the doorstep of my friend's house in Ottawa. The daisies on the welcome sign at the front door greeted me with warmth and reassurance.

The heat and humidity of Ontario in mid-July were a stark contrast to the temperate clime of the West Coast. Even Daisy 'Mo looked slightly dazed and confused on our walk that first morning, experiencing humidity for the first time in her life. Either that or she was concerned about the effect it would have on her normally well-behaved hairstyle.

What had once been very familiar territory to me now seemed curiously unfamiliar. As I rode my bicycle about town, I felt overwhelmed by traffic congestion, the noisy hustle and bustle of city life and unrelenting urban sprawl. The slow lane had been my comfortable home for over a year. As I ventured around the city, I didn't see a slow lane in sight.

It was a puzzling feeling to return to a place I'd called home for 10 years and know that I was the piece of the puzzle that didn't fit anymore. I had changed. Dramatically. For the better I thought, at least from my perspective.

My stay in Ottawa would be temporary, I knew that immediately. It would have its purpose, but I had no doubt the West Coast would call this wild daisy once again.

~

I had a home that wasn't on wheels and a roof that didn't leak. I wasn't in a parking lot or living on a street. I slept on a real bed. I was back amongst my close friends. My return to Ottawa certainly provided some comforts in the midst of some soul-searching discomfort.

The luxury was welcome after the many ups and downs of the previous months. My standards had clearly changed as much as I had. Suddenly, having access to a full-sized bathroom with a real flush toilet was very exciting.

Having landed back in Ottawa, very tired and not entirely on my terms, one of my first tasks was to find a way to reconcile the recent turn of events. This was a task that I often took with me on my evening walks with Daisy 'Mo. Thinking about anything but the unbearable heat and humidity was a welcome relief.

I knew that I couldn't change the circumstances. I could only change the way that I looked at them.

Yes, *Miss Daisy* had unexpectedly broken down. Yes, some things hadn't gone according to plan or expectation. Yes, I'd had some disappointments.

On the other hand, I'd enjoyed the biggest adventure of my lifetime and, in the process, had changed—everything.

After a few evenings of mulling, I realized something big. It wasn't important that *Miss Daisy* had died. What was most important was that I had taken the leap and put myself behind the driver's seat in the first place. I had finally found the courage to choose to live life differently and to drive off in the direction of my heart.

As with the rest of my life's roller coaster ride, I could gaze in my rear—view mirror and confidently exclaim, "Thanks *Miss Daisy*, you certainly gave me quite the ride."

~

I'd never told my Mom that I'd always wanted to be a bartender at some point. I figured I'd already given her enough to deal with for one lifetime. Yet, it was another one of my dreams, right up there with being a backup dancer for Madonna.

By the way Madonna, I'm still waiting for your call.

Bartending seemed like such a fun job to me, as if I'd be getting paid to be at a party. I simply *had* to give it a try.

As wondrously as *Miss Daisy* had allowed me to fulfil my truck-driving dream, my return to Ottawa would allow me to fulfil my bartender's dream.

Sure, I wanted to serve drinks, but my primary interest was to enjoy the social aspect of the job. Lucky me, I found the perfect place where I was able to combine fun, people and one of my lifelong loves, coffee.

I got a job as a barista at a local coffeehouse called Bridgehead. Surrounded by coffee beans and happy people high on caffeine, it was also the closest thing to being back on the West Coast that I would find in Ottawa. Even if I was the most 'senior' barista amongst the rest of the younger staff, I felt at home there.

It was one of the best jobs I've had in my lifetime. And I've had many, roughly 39 at last count, which includes my brief entrepreneurial stint trying to sell cucumbers door-to-door when I was seven. Hey, a wild daisy doesn't like to stay in the same place for too long. Life is far more fun when it gets to grow a bit here, a bit there and a bit everywhere.

I got to make fancy drinks and chat with customers. I got to know some of the locals in the community and I made some new friends. Plus I got to drink free coffee all day!

Most importantly however, I had the serendipitous opportunity to experience a spectrum of humanity that I wouldn't have had otherwise. I met coffee drinkers, latte lovers, smiley folks and grumpy bears. I cleaned up after messy people and meticulous people. I served tippers and non-tippers, the wealthy and the homeless. I greeted humourous people and humourless people. I witnessed people who can patiently wait in line and those who absolutely cannot. I met respectful people and some less-than-respectful people, including the customer who not so discretely showed me his middle finger when I sought to clarify his drink order. I watched conscientious folks carefully recycling and composting their leftovers and others who took 17 more napkins than they actually needed or used.

My one year as a barista had taught me more about people than I'd learned in my entire lifetime. Coffee simply provided the common grounds of the experience. The remaining pieces came together and reflected this complex thing we call humanity, which I found fascinating, and sometimes annoying, to observe on a daily basis.

It was also at Bridgehead that I met Rolph who is arguably one of the biggest sources of wisdom I've ever met.

Rolph was a regular at Bridgehead, he would stop by three or four times each day. Everyone in the area knew of Rolph because he spent his time walking the neighbourhood streets, stopping in at the local shops to chat or be helpful. Each night he'd head home to his assisted-living apartment and be back on the streets first thing the following morning.

You can't miss Rolph as he meanders on his walkabouts. He wears a bright orange baseball cap with his name embroidered on the front and walks slowly with the assistance of two walking poles. He carries a backpack, as well as a shopping bag dangled around his neck inside which he keeps flyers, magazines or recipes that he likes to share. Sometimes I'd see him while out walking dogs from the local grooming salon. Rolph was also proud to be the Chief Volunteer Dog-Poop-Picker-Upper of the neighbourhood.

Rolph simply likes to help others. Whenever he visited Bridgehead, he would help clear tables or offer us a magazine or recipe. I'm sure he did the same thing in every other shop he visited daily.

I never saw Rolph without his trademark smile and I never once heard him complain.

His life provided a provocative contrast in a neighbourhood of fancy homes in which many are 'living the dream'. Rolph, however, lives the kind of life that most people only ever dream about. He's genuinely happy. He lives a life of meaning and purpose. He makes a difference to the world around him.

Rolph's approach was simple.

Help others. Care. Live with purpose. Give. Be yourself. Live simply. Share your gift. Spread joy. Walk every day. Be loving and kind.

And drink plenty of coffee. Sometimes tea.

This is really important stuff to know and thanks to Rolph I'll never forget it.

~

Fall and winter passed quickly. When spring arrived, I knew that my time in Ottawa would soon be over.

A rather gypsy-like lifestyle remained my norm while in town. Never wanting to feel too settled, I moved four times in less than a year. Thankfully, I travelled light and all of my possessions could easily and quickly be relocated in one carload.

After my last move, I decided the next one would take me back out west. I could hear my heart telling me that it was time to go.

All the signs were pointing in that direction as well. Literally. While driving around Ottawa one day I happened across a huge street sign for Nanaimo Drive, with an arrow pointing west. *Okay, I get the big hint, thank you.*

I only needed enough money for rent and airfare. I also needed to find a place to live in Nanaimo and a job in a town that is known to have a high unemployment rate.

First, I scrounged enough money for airfare. Check!

Second, I found a place to live relatively easily. Check!

Then I contacted a downtown coffee shop that I'd frequented when I'd previously been in Nanaimo. Thank goodness for the barista experience I'd gained in Ottawa as I was quickly offered a job. Check! All of my bases of life were covered.

This time the path to Nanaimo offered no resistance to my return.

On August 3, 2011, a warm, sunshine-filled day, I (with Daisy 'Mo) arrived back in Nanaimo. A friend met me at the ferry to take me to my new apartment. Fresh air, ocean and mountains lined the highway as we drove and happiness filled my heart and soul.

I knew in an instant that I had found my way back home, to stay.

chapter 64

The Road Ahead

As I sit at the kitchen table, gazing at the ocean and mountains, an eagle floats on a thermal in the distance. It is a peaceful and powerful scene, one that humbles me with its beauty and sense of possibility. Ironically, these were all the things that I hadn't discovered in my own life—inner peace, my personal power and beauty, or my own possibilities—before embarking on my journey of the heart. My view of life has certainly changed over the past couple of years.

I took a long, meandering road to finally arrive here, a physical and spiritual home that makes my heart sing. Fortunately, destiny is always there waiting for us no matter what path we choose to take or how long it takes to get there.

As I glance out the window towards the east, I realize how far I am from where I'd begun. Not that I know where the beginning was anyways. One thing, or perhaps one daisy, simply kept leading to another. How do you ever really know where a journey began or where it ends?

Certainly my current life bears little resemblance to the one I used to have. I am very grateful for that.

I now have a minimalist lifestyle: few belongings, no house, no car. Instead, I have freedom and flexibility. I live in a place that I love. I enjoy a lifestyle that reflects what I value the most. I choose to do work that I love. I am surrounded by ocean, mountains and Nanaimo bars. New friendships have arrived to replace the ones that didn't feel right anymore.

I discovered confidence, strength and resourcefulness that I didn't know I had. The unknowns of life no longer scare me. Instead, faith, hope and courage have taken their place. And somewhere along the way the real Me was set free.

I am happy, truly happy.

I am finally standing in a life that *feels right*. I can finally look at myself and my surroundings and say, *This is me. This is my life!*

It wasn't always easy but it was certainly necessary. Any of the challenges or obstacles I faced were certainly less trying to deal with than living an unfulfilled, unauthentic life and watching my soul slowly die in the process.

I'd wanted an adventure and I'd certainly had one. I'd wanted to follow my heart wherever it would take me and I'd certainly done that too. Somewhere along the way I discovered that following my heart *is* the adventure. And it's an adventure that I intend to continue until the day that I die.

I can now check a few dreams off of my 'bucket list' too. I've lived the truck driver and bartender dream. I've travelled across Canada and now live in British Columbia, a province I'd wanted to live in ever since I was in my teens. And now I've finished the book that I promised I'd write when I first hit the road with *Miss Daisy*.

I don't know what lies on the road ahead and that's okay. I'm prepared for the unexpected. I'm sure there will be more adventures, more surprises and more daisies waiting around the next bend.

~

I am watching the eagle in flight as it moves effortlessly and gracefully across the horizon, in complete harmony with its world. It doesn't fight the wind, it flows with it. Through my binoculars, I see this big brave bird make a large swooping turn and land on the top of a nearby tree. It's a rare scene to behold and one that has my full attention. In fact, it's as if the eagle wants me to pay attention. To notice *something*.

It's a sunny, clear day. The ocean waters glisten and dance in the sunlight, against the panoramic backdrop of the snow-capped mountains on the mainland coast. It's the most beautiful view I've ever seen in my life. And I'm feeling the most beautiful feelings I've ever felt in my life.

This is where I am. I followed my heart and *this* is where it brought me.

Thank you God. Thank you Santiago. And, of course, thank you daisies.

About the Author

Heather Pardon is an adventurist in life. True to her "Wild Daisy" nickname, she's taken a meandering road in life but somehow managed to finally arrive at a place where she's happy to be.

It only took 40-plus years, a series of botched relationships, a few years of psychotherapy, approximately 56 self-help books, one nervous breakdown, several servings of carrot cake, a complete life overhaul and a cross-country trip in a daisy-covered RV...and more... but at least she can say that the journey was never boring.

Her "daisy-like" career path which has included stints as a chef, fundraiser, personal trainer, life coach, bed and breakfast owner and more has afforded her the opportunity to study the spectrum of one of her true passions, human nature.

Now she does what she loves most. She is an author and an inspirational public speaker. Heather's goal is simple – to help others learn to follow their heart and live an adventurous life that is fun, inspired and feels good.

Heather happily lives in Nanaimo, British Columbia with her Jack Russell Terrier, Daisy 'Mo, and a stash of Nanaimo bars.

You can visit Heather's website at www.wilddaisy.ca

Acknowledgements

I was never truly alone on this journey, not while I was adventuring with *Miss Daisy* nor while I was working on completing this book. I am most grateful to the many wild daisy spirits who helped and supported me on my way.

A big daisy thank you to Tara Taylor and Pat Armstrong, two angels and friends who gifted me with one of the most important lessons in life, to "just say yes". To my good friend, Peggy McColl, thank you for all of your tremendous support and encouragement, fun and laughter and for inspiring me to dream big dreams. And a huge thank you for letting me stay with you AND park *Miss Daisy* in your driveway for three weeks after I'd sold my house.

I owe a standing ovation to my editor, Sheila Ascroft, whose editorial skills and ability to prod my writing, I greatly appreciated. A bouquet of daisies goes to Lindsay Wickware who designed a cover and layout that I absolutely love.

Thanks to all who agreed to have their names and stories included in this book. It simply wouldn't have been the same without you.

A huge thanks to my brother, Ray, who helped me out in innumerable ways over the years. And to the rest of my family for just letting me be who I am.

I met many new friends while travelling this daisy-lined road in life.

It's been truly magical and I'm very grateful for all of the experiences and wonderful friendships I've enjoyed while following daisies.

And, of course, thank you to the gang at the Magical Dream Place Headquarters, whoever and wherever you are! I really love and appreciate the work that you do.

And, most of all, thank *you* for being an inspiration.

Peace, Love and Daisies,

Heather

Made in the USA
Charleston, SC
07 November 2013